BERENSON'S
ITALIAN PICTURES
OF THE RENAISSANCE

PHAIDON PRESS

TITIAN: Detail from *The Worship of Venus*. Prado, Madrid.

ITALIAN PICTURES OF THE RENAISSANCE

A LIST OF THE PRINCIPAL ARTISTS
AND THEIR WORKS
WITH AN INDEX OF PLACES

BY

BERNARD BERENSON

VENETIAN SCHOOL
IN TWO VOLUMES

VOL. II

WITH 705 ILLUSTRATIONS

PHAIDON

PHAIDON PRESS LIMITED, 5 CROMWELL PLACE, LONDON SW7

PUBLISHED IN THE UNITED STATES OF AMERICA BY PHAIDON PUBLISHERS, INC.

AND DISTRIBUTED BY PRAEGER PUBLISHERS, INC.

111 FOURTH AVENUE, NEW YORK, N.Y. 10003

ISBN 0 7148 1486 5

MADE IN GREAT BRITAIN

VENETIAN PICTURES
OF THE RENAISSANCE

629. GIORGIONE: *Judith (cut down at the sides)*. Hermitage, Leningrad.

631. MASTER OF THE THREE AGES (EARLY GIORGIONE?): *Bust of Woman.*
Royal Collections, Hampton Court.
Reproduced by gracious permission of H.M. the Queen

630. MASTER OF THE THREE AGES (EARLY GIORGIONE?):
Detail from the Three Ages of Man. Pitti, Florence.

632. MASTER OF THE THREE AGES (EARLY GIORGIONE?): *Concert*. Royal Collections, Hampton Court.
Reproduced by gracious permission of H.M. the Queen

634. GIORGIONE, AFTER GIOVANNI BELLINI: *Christ carrying the Cross.*
I. S. Gardner Museum, Boston (Mass.). *Early work.*

633. GIOVANNI BELLINI: *Christ carrying the Cross.*
Formerly Comte de Pourtalès, Paris.

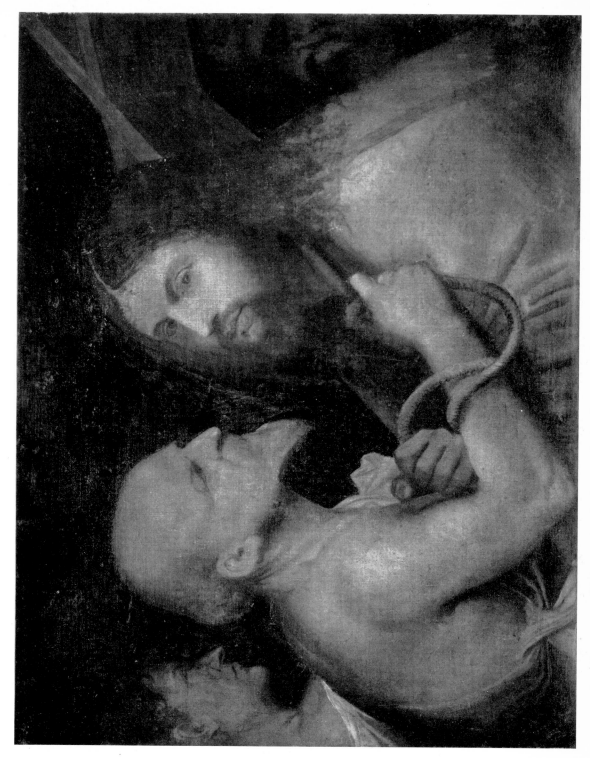

635. GIORGIONE: *Christ carrying the Cross and other figures. Scuola di S. Rocco, Venice. Late work, in ruined condition.*

636. GIORGIONE: *Judgement of Solomon* (*detail*). Uffizi, Florence.

637. GIORGIONE: *Predella panel: the 'Benson' Holy Family*. National Gallery of Art, Washington.

639. GIORGIONE: *Bust of Youth, from the Palazzo Giustiniani.*
Staatliche Museen, Berlin.

638. GIORGIONE: *Madonna with Liberale and Francis (detail).*
S. Liberale, Castelfranco.

641. GIORGIONE: *Epiphany (detail)*. National Gallery, London

640. GIORGIONE: *Trial of Moses (detail)*. Uffizi, Florence.

642. GIORGIONE: *Predella panel: Epiphany*. National Gallery, London.

643. GIORGIONE: *Detail from Plate 642.*

644. GIORGIONE: *The 'Allendale' Nativity (finished by Titian)*. National Gallery of Art, Washington.

645. GIORGIONE: 'Laura' (cut down). Kunsthistorisches Museum, Vienna. 1506.
646. DAVID TENIERS THE YOUNGER: Copy of 'Laura' before mutilation (detail from the Gallery of Archduke Leopold Wilhelm in Brussels). Prado, Madrid. After 1659.

647. GIORGIONE: *Portrait of ? Ariosto*. Metropolitan Museum of Art, New York.

648. GIORGIONE: *Gipsy and Soldier*. Accademia, Venice.

651. GIORGIONE: *Madonna with Anthony of Padua and Roch (unfinished)*. Prado, Madrid.

652. GIORGIONE: *Detail from Plate 651.*

653. GIORGIONE: *Bust of Courtesan.* Formerly Lord Melchett, London.

655. GIORGIONE: *Bust of Shepherd with pipe.* Royal Collections,
Hampton Court.
Reproduced by gracious permission of H.M. the Queen

654. GIORGIONE: *Bust of Youth as Sebastian.*
Kunsthistorisches Museum, Vienna.

656. GIORGIONE: 'The three Philosophers' (finished by Sebastiano del Piombo). Kunsthistorisches Museum, Vienna.

657. GIORGIONE: *Sleeping Venus* (*finished by Titian*). Gemäldegalerie, Dresden.

658. GIORGIONE: 'Fête champêtre'. Louvre, Paris.

659. GIORGIONE: *Christ and the Adulteress (detail)*. Corporation Art Gallery, Glasgow.

660. GIORGIONE: *Christ and the Adulteress* (*detail*). Corporation Art Gallery, Glasgow.

661. CARIANI: *Copy of Giorgione's Christ and the Adulteress before its mutilation. Accademia Carrara, Bergamo.*

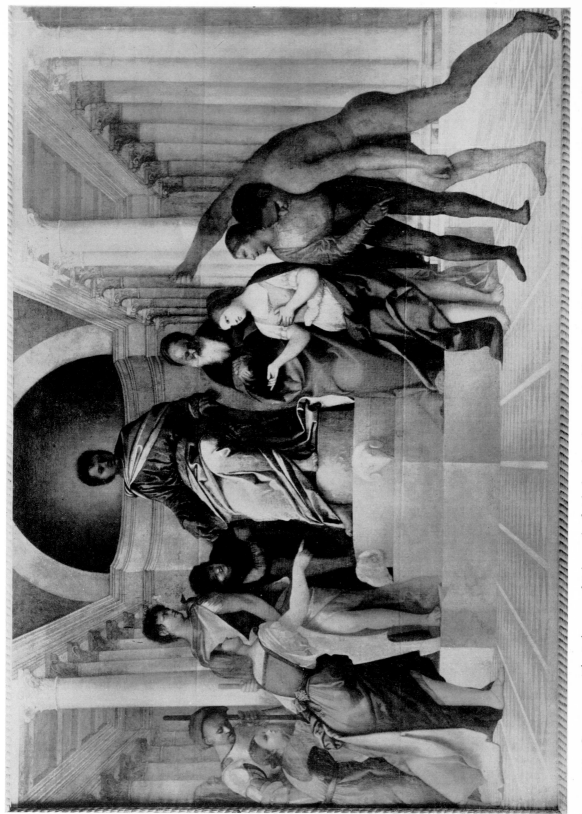

662. Giorgione: *The Judgement of Solomon (unfinished and partly overpainted)*. Bankes Collection, Kingston Lacy, Wimborne (Dorset).

663. Giorgione (partly): *Apollo and Daphne*. Seminario, Venice.

664. GIORGIONESQUE PAINTER: *Allegory of Chastity*. Rijksmuseum, Amsterdam.

665. GIORGIONESQUE FURNITURE PAINTER: *Leda and the Swan*. Museo Civico, Padua.

666. GIORGIONESQUE FURNITURE PAINTER: *Pastoral Scene*. Museo Civico, Padua.

667. Giorgionesque furniture painter: *Allegory of Time*. D. Phillips Memorial Gallery, Washington.

668. Giorgionesque furniture painter: *Landscape with Nymph and Cupid*.
National Gallery of Art, Washington.

669-670. GIORGIONESQUE FURNITURE PAINTER (EARLY TITIAN?): *The birth of Adonis; the myth of Erysichthon.* Museo Civico, Padua.

671-672. GIORGIONESQUE FURNITURE PAINTER: *Landscape with old Man and Deer; Landscape with Shepherds and Cavaliers.* Marquis de Ganay, Paris.

673. GIORGIONESQUE PAINTER: *Landscape with Soldier and Woman seated with Child.*
Marquess of Northampton, Compton Wynyates (Warwicks.).

674. GIORGIONESQUE PAINTER: *Landscape with two Soldiers and Dragon.* Formerly John McIlhenny,
Philadelphia (Pa.).

675. DAVID TENIERS THE YOUNGER: *Copy of Giorgione's lost 'Finding of Paris'*.
Formerly Ch. Loeser, Florence.

676. *Copy of Giorgione's lost 'Judgement of Paris'*. Formerly Enrico Albuzio, Venice.

GIORGON

VERO RITRATTO DE GIORGONE DE CASTEL FRANCO
da luy fatto come lo celebra il libro del VASARI.

677   678

677. David Teniers the Younger: *Copy of Giorgione's 'Self-portrait' (detail from the Gallery of Archduke Leopold Wilhelm in Brussels). Prado, Madrid. After 1659.*
678. Wenzel Hollar: *Engraving after Giorgione's 'Self-portrait as David'. 1650.*

679. Palma Vecchio: *Version of Giorgione's 'Self-portrait'*. Museum, Budapest.

680. Palma Vecchio: *Version of Giorgione's 'Self-portrait as David'*. Landesmuseum, Brunswick.

Giorgione pinxit   *Dom. Cunego scalpsit 1773*

Ex Tabula Romæ in Ædibus Burghesianis affervata

681. Domenico Cunego: *Engraving after Giorgione's 'Lovers'. 1773.*

682. GIORGIONESQUE PAINTER: *Bust of Archer*.
National Gallery of Scotland, Edinburgh.

683. AFTER GIORGIONE: *Warrior and Page*.
Major Howard, Castle Howard (Yorks.).

684. PALMA VECCHIO, AFTER GIORGIONE:
Youth in fox-fur. Alte Pinakothek, Munich.

685. PALMA VECCHIO, AFTER GIORGIONE:
'*Il Bravo*'. Kunsthistorisches Museum, Vienna.

686. ALESSANDRO OLIVERIO: *Roch between Jerome and Sebastian*, Sacristy, S. Maria della Salute, Venice.

687. ALESSANDRO OLIVERIO: *Youth of the Cornaro Family*. National Gallery of Ireland, Dublin. *Signed*.

688. ALESSANDRO OLIVERIO: *Bust of Gentleman*. Dr. A. Schrafl, Zurich.

689. ALESSANDRO OLIVERIO: *Bust of Man with hand on parapet*. Homeless. *Late work*.

690. ALESSANDRO OLIVERIO: *Eve*. Galleria Borghese, Rome.

691. DOMENICO MANCINI: *Madonna with Angel playing lute*. Duomo, Lendinara (Rovigo).
Signed and dated 1511.

692. DOMENICO MANCINI: *Madonna with Baptist and Peter*. Conte Carlo Gamba, Florence.

693. DOMENICO MANCINI: *Sacra Conversazione with Joseph, Catherine, Sebastian and Donor*. Louvre, Paris.

694. DOMENICO MANCINI: *Bust of lute player*. Kunsthistorisches Museum, Vienna.

695. DOMENICO MANCINI: *The Lovers*. Gemäldegalerie, Dresden.

696. DOMENICO MANCINI: *Tomyris plunging Cyrus' head in the Vessel of Blood*. Formerly Mallman Collection, Blaschkow (Silesia).

697. SEBASTIANO DEL PIOMBO: *Adoration of the Shepherds*. Fitzwilliam Museum, Cambridge.

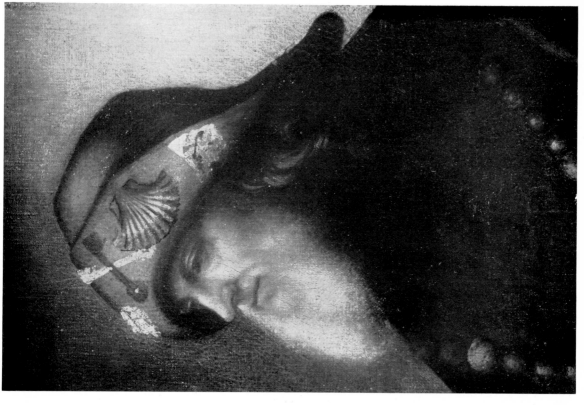

699. SEBASTIANO DEL PIOMBO: *Sinibald* (*detail of organ-shutter*).
S. Bartolomeo a Rialto, Venice. *1507–9*.

698. SEBASTIANO DEL PIOMBO: *Louis of Toulouse* (*detail of organ-shutter*).
S. Bartolomeo a Rialto, Venice. *1507–9*.

700. SEBASTIANO DEL PIOMBO: *The closed organ-shutters: Bartholomew and Sebastian*. S. Bartolomeo a
Rialto, Venice. *1507-9*.

701. SEBASTIANO DEL PIOMBO: *John Chrysostom surrounded by six Saints (Baptist and Liberale laid in by Giorgione)*. S. Giovanni Crisostomo, Venice. *1508–10.*

703. Sebastiano del Piombo: *Bust of Man with forked beard and soft hat.* Homeless.

702. Sebastiano del Piombo: *Young Woman represented as Wise Virgin.* National Gallery of Art, Washington.

704. SEBASTIANO DEL PIOMBO: *Death of Adonis*. Uffizi, Florence.

705. Sebastiano del Piombo: *Fresco: Juno.* Farnesina, Rome. *1511.*

707. Sebastiano del Piombo: *Cardinal Ciocchi del Monte Sansovino with a monkey.*
National Gallery of Ireland, Dublin.

706. SEBASTIANO DEL PIOMBO: *Fresco: Procne and Philomela transformed into birds.* Farnesina, Rome. *1511.*

708. SEBASTIANO DEL PIOMBO: *Young Roman Woman (so-called 'Dorothea').*
Staatliche Museen, Berlin.

709. SEBASTIANO DEL PIOMBO: *The Raising of Lazarus (detail)*. National Gallery, London. *Signed. 1519.*

710. Sebastiano del Piombo: *Christ on the way to Calvary*. Prado, Madrid.

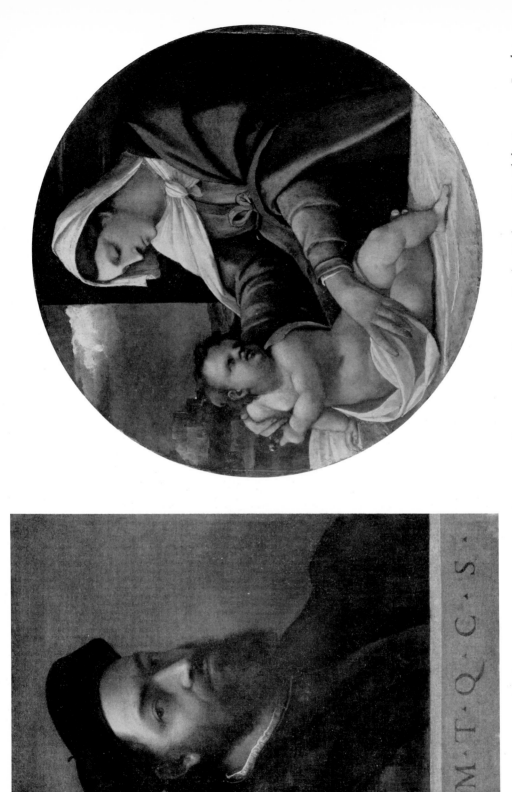

711. Sebastiano del Piombo: *Bust of Prelate*. Conte Vittorio Cini, Venice.   712. Sebastiano del Piombo: *Tondo: Madonna*. Mr. Philip Pouncey, London.

713. Sebastiano del Piombo: *Martyrdom of Agatha. Pitti, Florence. Signed and dated 1520.*

714. Sebastiano del Piombo: *Conte Federico da Bozzolo*. S. H. Kress Foundation, New York. *ca 1520*.

715. Sebastiano del Piombo: *Andrea Doria*. Principe Doria-Pamphilj, Rome. *1526*.

716. Sebastiano del Piombo: *Christ carrying the Cross*. Hermitage, Leningrad. *1537*.

717. Sebastiano del Piombo: *Pietà*. S. Salvador, Ubeda (Andalusia).
1537-9.

718. Sebastiano del Piombo: *Birth of the Virgin (detail)*. S. Maria del Popolo, Rome. *Begun in 1532 (?)*
and finished by Francesco Salviati after 1554.

720. MORTO DA FELTRE: *Fresco: Christ appearing to Anthony Abbot and Lucy.*
Sacristy, Ognissanti, Feltre. 1522.

719. MORTO DA FELTRE: *Madonna with Stephen and Liberale.*
Staatliche Museen, Berlin. *Signed and dated 1511.*

722. CARIANI: *Madonna in Landscape*. Hermitage, Leningrad.

721. CARIANI: *Madonna reading and view of the 'Piazzetta'*.
Ashmolean Museum, Oxford. ca 1510.

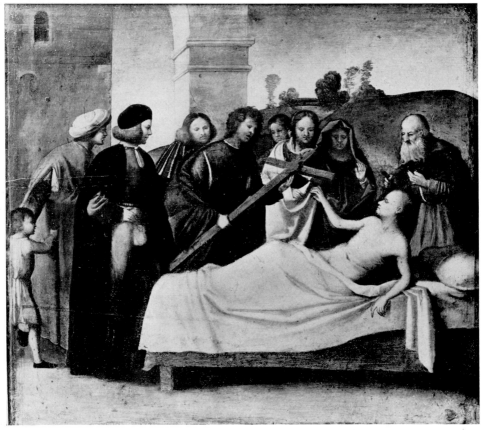

723-724. CARIANI: *The Finding of the True Cross; the first Miracle of the True Cross.*
Homeless.

725. CARIANI: *Sacra Conversazione with Jerome, Francis and Infant Baptist.*
Museo Poldi Pezzoli, Milan. *Signed.*

726. CARIANI: *Adoration of the Shepherds.* Homeless.

727. CARIANI: *Madonna with Peter*. Galleria Borghese, Rome.

728. CARIANI: *Young Men and Women of the Albani Family*. Conte Roncalli, Bergamo.
Signed and dated 1519.

729. CARIANI: *Resurrection with Jerome, Baptist, Ottaviano Visconti and his Wife*. Conte Paolo Gerli, Milan.
Signed and dated 1520.

750. ANDREA PREVITALI: *Baptist in the Wilderness.*
Gallery of Fine Arts, Columbus (Ohio). *Signed and dated 1521.*

749. ANDREA PREVITALI: *Christ in the Garden.* Brera, Milan.
Signed and dated 1513.

751. Andrea Previtali: *Preaching of Baptist, and Baptism of Christ. Homeless.*

752. ANDREA PREVITALI: *The Crossing of the Red Sea*. Accademia, Venice.

753. ANDREA PREVITALI: *Madonna with two Saints, Casotti and his Wife*. Accademia Carrara, Bergamo.

754. ANDREA PREVITALI: *Family group against coastal landscape.* Conte Moroni, Bergamo.

755. LORENZO LOTTO: *A Maiden's Dream*. National Gallery of Art, Washington.

756. LORENZO LOTTO: *Venus in landscape*. Homeless.

757. Lorenzo Lotto: *Bishop Bernardo de' Rossi di Berceto*. Museo Nazionale, Naples. *1505*.

758. LORENZO LOTTO: *Bust of Youth against white Curtain*. Kunsthistorisches Museum, Vienna.

759. LORENZO LOTTO: *Jerome in the Wilderness*. Louvre, Paris. *Signed and dated 1506.*

760. Lorenzo Lotto: *Peter Martyr and Vitus (detail of polyptych)*.
Pinacoteca Comunale, Recanati. *Signed and dated 1508.*

761. LORENZO LOTTO: *Madonna adoring the Child with Infant Baptist, Francis, Jerome and Catherine.*
Formerly Count Sigismund Puslowski, Cracow. *Signed.*

762. LORENZO LOTTO: *Half-length portrait of young Man holding a 'Petrarchino'*. Homeless.

763. Lorenzo Lotto: *Madonna with Alexander, Barbara, James, Dominic, Mark, Catherine, Stephen, Augustine, Baptist and Sebastian.* S. Bartolomeo, Bergamo. *Signed and dated 1516.*

764. LORENZO LOTTO: *Predella of the S. Bartolomeo Altarpiece: The stoning of Stephen (detail).*
Accademia Carrara, Bergamo. *1516.*

765. LORENZO LOTTO: *Predella of the S. Bartolomeo Altarpiece: Miracle of Dominic (detail).*
Accademia Carrara, Bergamo. *1516.*

766. LORENZO LOTTO: *Susanna and the Elders*. Contini Bonacossi Collection, Florence.
Signed and dated 1517.

767. LORENZO LOTTO: *Christ taking leave of His Mother, with Elisabetta Rota as Donor.*
Staatliche Museen, Berlin. *Signed and dated 1521.*

768. LORENZO LOTTO: *Messer Marsilio and his Bride*. Prado, Madrid. *Signed and dated 1523*.

769. LORENZO LOTTO: *Fresco: Clare taking her vow*. Oratorio Suardi, Trescore (Bergamo). *1524*.

770. LORENZO LOTTO: *Creation*. Intarsia on choir-stall, S. Maria Maggiore, Bergamo. *1523-33.*

771-772. LORENZO LOTTO: *Two Allegories*. Intarsias on benches, S. Maria Maggiore, Bergamo. *1523-33.*

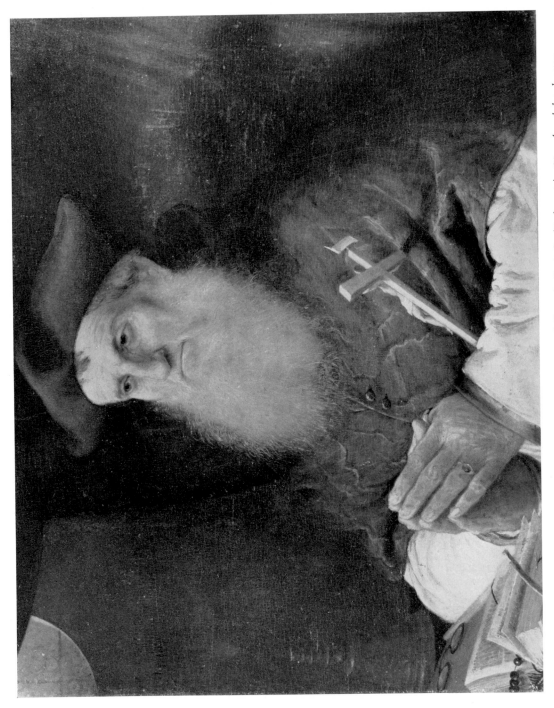

773. LORENZO LOTTO: *Bishop Tommaso Negri. Monastero delle Paludi, Split (Dalmatia). Signed and dated 1527.*

774. Lorenzo Lotto: *Sacra Conversazione*. Kunsthistorisches Museum, Vienna.

775. LORENZO LOTTO: *The Triumph of Chastity*. Palazzo Rospigliosi Pallavicini, Rome. *Signed*.

776. LORENZO LOTTO: *Ceiling: Allegory of the Arts of the Quadrivium*.
Formerly Baron von Hadeln, Florence.

777. Lorenzo Lotto: *Crucifixion*. S. Maria in Telusiano, Monte San Giusto. *Signed and dated 1531*.

778. LORENZO LOTTO: *Visitation*. Civica Pinacoteca, Jesi. *Signed and dated 153?0.*

779. LORENZO LOTTO: *Jerome in his Study (after Dürer).*
Zocca Collection, Rome.

780-781. LORENZO LOTTO: *The Saint Lucy Altarpiece: Lucy before her Judges, and detail of Predella with episodes from her Life*. Civica Pinacoteca, Jesi. *Signed and dated 1532.*

782. LORENZO LOTTO: *Recognition of the Holy Child*. Louvre, Paris.

783. LORENZO LOTTO: *Apollo asleep on Parnassus*. Museum, Budapest.

784. LORENZO LOTTO: *The Madonna of the Rosary*. S. Domenico, Cingoli (Macerata).
Signed and dated 1539.

786. Lorenzo Lotto: *Half-length portrait of Astronomer.* Homeless.

785. Lorenzo Lotto: *Half-length portrait of Gentleman with large Book (Baldassarre Soranzo?).* Homeless. *Signed and dated 1541.*

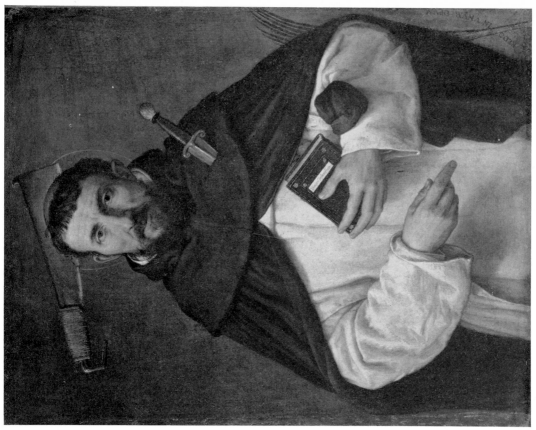

788. LORENZO LOTTO: *Half-length portrait of a Dominican Friar as Peter Martyr.*
Fogg Art Museum, Cambridge (Mass.).

787. LORENZO LOTTO: *Half-length portrait of Fra Gregorio da Vicenza
with Crucifixion in background. Homeless. 1546.*

789. Lorenzo Lotto: *Jerome in the Wilderness*. Homeless. *Signed*.

790. Lorenzo Lotto: *Entombment*. Homeless.

791. Lorenzo Lotto: *Presentation in the Temple (unfinished)*. Palazzo Apostolico, Loreto. *ca 1555*.

792. ANTONIO DA FAENZA: *Closed organ-shutters: Annunciation with Isaiah and Luke.*
Palazzo Apostolico, Loreto. *1514.*

793. ANTONIO DA FAENZA: *Madonna with six Saints; in predella: Annunciation and Pietà.*
S. Benedetto, Norcia.

794. GIOVANNI DA ASOLA: *Madonna with Louis of France and Elizabeth of Hungary.*
Formerly Hon. G. A. F. Cavendish Bentinck, London.

795. GIOVANNI DA ASOLA: *Supper at Emmaus*. Saint-Louis-en-l'Ile, Paris.

796. GIOVANNI DA ASOLA: *Female Saint and Warrior Saint with Infant Baptist*. Lee of Fareham Collection, University of London.

797. GIOVANNI DA ASOLA: *Last Supper*. Pinacoteca Querini Stampalia, Venice.

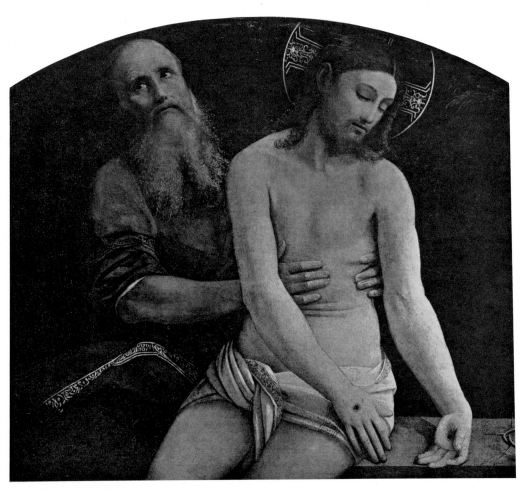

798. BERNARDINO DA ASOLA: *Dead Christ upheld by Joseph of Arimathea*. Homeless.

799. Giovanni and Bernardino da Asola: *Organ-shutter from S. Michele, Murano: Benedict enthroned, with two Monks*. Museo Correr, Venice. *1526*.

800. GIOVANNI AND BERNARDINO DA ASOLA: *Organ-shutter from S. Michele, Murano:*
Michael hurling Satan down to Hell. Museo Correr, Venice. 1526.

801. GIOVANNI AND BERNARDINO DA ASOLA: *Organ-shutter from S. Michele, Murano: Assumption*. Museo Correr, Venice. *1526*.

802. GIOVANNI AND BERNARDINO DA ASOLA: *Detail from Plate 801.*

803. BERNARDINO DA ASOLA: *Holy Family.* Homeless.

804. GIROLAMO SAVOLDO: *Madonna with Baptist and Jerome*. National Gallery of Ireland, Dublin.

805. GIROLAMO SAVOLDO: *Entombment*. Museum, Budapest.

807. GIROLAMO SAVOLDO: *Bust of a Man.*
Formerly Henry Doetsch Collection, London. *ca* 1530.

806. GIROLAMO SAVOLDO: *Bust of a Man.*
Formerly Earl of Crawford, Balcarres (Fife). *ca* 1515.

808. GIROLAMO SAVOLDO: *Madonna adoring Child, with a male and a female Donor.* Royal Collections, Hampton Court. *1527.*
Reproduced by gracious permission of H.M. the Queen

809. GIROLAMO SAVOLDO: *Rest on the Flight, with Venice in background.*
Conte A. Castelbarco Albani, Milan.

810. GIROLAMO SAVOLDO: *Portrait of a Lady as Saint Margaret.* Pinacoteca Capitolina, Rome.

811. GIROLAMO SAVOLDO: *Detail from Plate 812.*

812. GIROLAMO SAVOLDO: *Madonna in Glory with Peter, Dominic, Paul and Jerome below.*
Brera, Milan. *ca 1535.*

813. Girolamo Savoldo: *Transfiguration*. Uffizi, Florence.

814. GIROLAMO SAVOLDO: *Adoration of the Shepherds (detail)*. Pinacoteca Martinengo, Brescia.

815. GIROLAMO SAVOLDO: *Elija fed by ravens and his Disciples witnessing his Ascension in a chariot of fire.*
S. H. Kress Foundation, New York.

818. Girolamo Savoldo: *Nativity*. Albertini Collection, Rome.

819. GIROLAMO SAVOLDO: *Matthew and the Angel*. Metropolitan Museum, New York.

820. GIOVANNI DA MEL: *Madonna with James and Liberale*. Sacristy, Chiesa Arcipretale, Lentiai (Belluno).
Signed.

821. GIOVANNI DA MEL: *Madonna with Bishop Saint and Victor*. Chiesa Arcipretale, Mel (Belluno).
Signed and dated 1530.

822. MARCELLO FOGOLINO: *Epiphany; Annunciation in predella*. Museo Civico, Vicenza. *Signed.*

823. MARCELLO FOGOLINO: *Detail from Plate 822.*

825. MARCELLO FOGOLINO: *Nativity*. Museo di Castelvecchio, Verona. *Signed.*

824. MARCELLO FOGOLINO: *Madonna*. Formerly Guggenheim Collection, Venice.

826. MARCELLO FOGOLINO: *Frescoes on Façade*. Castello del Buonconsiglio, Trent. *1531*.

827. MARCELLO FOGOLINO: *Madonna and six Saints*. Staatliche Museen, Berlin. *Signed*.

828. MARCELLO FOGOLINO: *Francis between Baptist and Daniel*. Duomo, Pordenone.

829. Luca Monverde: *Madonna with Roch, Gervasius, Protasius and Sebastian.*
S. Maria delle Grazie, Udine. *1522.*

830. Pellegrino da San Daniele: *Madonna with eight Saints, Putti and music-making Angels.*
Chiesa Parrocchiale, Osoppo (Udine). *1495*.

831. PELLEGRINO DA SAN DANIELE: *Frescoes in Apse (detail)*. S. Antonio, San Daniele del Friuli.
Signed and dated 1498.

832. PELLEGRINO DA SAN DANIELE: *Joseph and Worshipper*. Duomo, Udine. *1501*.

835. PELLEGRINO DA SAN DANIELE: *Annunciation*. Museo Civico, Udine. *Signed and dated 1519.*

836. PELLEGRINO DA SAN DANIELE: *Sebastian, Job and Roch (fresco).* S. Antonio, San Daniele del Friuli.
1515-22.

837. Pellegrino da San Daniele: *Angel (fresco)*. S. Antonio, San Daniele del Friuli. *1515-22*.

838. GIOVANNI BATTISTA GRASSI DA UDINE: *Madonna*. S. H. Kress Foundation, New York. *Signed*.

839. BERNARDINO LICINIO: *Holy Family with Magdalen.* Formerly Capt. R. Wyndham, Clouds (Salisbury, Wilts.). *Signed.*

840. BERNARDINO LICINIO: *Portrait of a Scholar.* Formerly Principe Chigi, Rome. *Signed.*

841. BERNARDINO LICINIO: *Portrait of a Lady.* Museum, Budapest. *Dated 1552.*

842. BERNARDINO LICINIO: *Family Group.* Royal Collections, Hampton Court. *1524.*
Reproduced by gracious permission of H.M. the Queen

843. BERNARDINO LICINIO: *An Artist and his Pupils*. Duke of Northumberland, Alnwick Castle (Northd.).

855. (?) PORDENONE: *Young Man looking up from reading Petrarch*. S. H. Kress Collection, H. M. De Young Memorial Museum, San Francisco (California).

856. Pordenone: *Transfiguration (from Collalto)*. Brera, Milan. *1511*.

858. PORDENONE: *Baptist and Jerome* (destroyed in 1917).
Castello, Collalto (Treviso). *1511.*

857. PORDENONE: *Prosdocimus and Peter (from Collalto).*
S. H. Kress Foundation, New York. *1511.*

860. PORDENONE: *Luke*. Museum, Budapest.

859. PORDENONE: *Mark*. Museum, Budapest.

861. PORDENONE: *Madonna with John the Baptist, Catherine, John the Evangelist and Peter.*
Chiesa Parrocchiale, Susegana (Treviso).

862. PORDENONE: *Madonna of Mercy between Christopher and Joseph* Duomo, Pordenone (Udine). *1516*.

863. PORDENONE: *Fresco: The Nailing to the Cross.* Duomo, Cremona. *1521.*

864. PORDENONE: *Fresco: Crucifixion (detail).* Duomo, Cremona. *1521.*

865. PORDENONE: *Fresco: Crucifixion (detail)*. Duomo, Cremona. *1521*.

866. PORDENONE: *Organ-shutter: The Conversion of Paul.* Duomo, Spilimbergo (Udine).
After 1524.

867. PORDENONE: *Triptych: Madonna and Angels between Lawrence and James, Anthony Abbot and Michael.*
S. Lorenzo, Varmo (Udine). *1526-30.*

868. PORDENONE: *Detail from Plate 867.*

869. PORDENONE: *Gothard enthroned between Roch and Sebastian*. Municipio, Pordenone (Udine). *1526*.

870. PORDENONE: *Cover of harpsichord: the wounded Satyr*. Sig.ra Adele de Maria Macchi, Rome.

871. PORDENONE: *Martin and Christopher with Suppliants (detail)*. S. Rocco, Venice. *1528*.

872. PORDENONE: *Panels from parapet of organ: Hermagoras before the Judge, Hermagoras flagellated, Fortunatus before Sebastes, Hermagoras baptizing through the prison window, Beheading of Hermagoras and Fortunatus.*
Sacristy, Duomo, Udine. *1527.*

873. PORDENONE: *Fresco on the ceiling: The Eternal Father*. Cappella Pallavicini, Chiesa dei Francescani, Cortemaggiore (Piacenza).

875. PORDENONE: *Lorenzo Giustiniani and six other Saints.* Accademia, Venice. *Signed and dated 1532.*

874. PORDENONE: *Dispute about the Immaculate Conception (from the Cappella Pallavicini, Cortemaggiore).* Museo Nazionale, Naples. *Just before 1529.*

876. FRANCESCO PAGANI, DA MILANO: *Adoration of the Shepherds and Marriage of Virgin above (detail).*
S. Martino, Conegliano (Treviso).

877. FRANCESCO PAGANI, DA MILANO: *Triptych: Roch between Sebastian and Nicholas.* Chiesa Parrocchiale,
Caneva di Sacile (Udine). *Signed and dated 1517.*

878. Francesco Pagani, da Milano: *Baptism*. S. Giovanni Battista, Vittorio Veneto. *1529*.

879. FRANCESCO PAGANI, DA MILANO: *Madonna with Bartholomew, Andrew and Angels (from Collalto).*
Museo Civico, Treviso. *Signed and dated 1538.*

880. FRANCESCO PAGANI, DA MILANO: *Organ shutters: Agatha, Andrew, Peter and Catherine.*
Duomo di Serravalle, Vittorio Veneto. *1528-32.*

881. POMPONIO AMALTEO: *Abraham and Isaac (detail of ceiling).*
S. Giovanni, Gemona (Udine). *1533.*

882. POMPONIO AMALTEO: *Sebastian with Roch, Cosmas, Damian and Apollonia.*
Duomo, San Vito al Tagliamento. *Signed and dated 1533.*

883. POMPONIO AMALTEO: *Flight into Egypt.* Duomo, Pordenone (Udine). *Signed and dated 1565.*

884. POMPONIO AMALTEO: *Entombment*. Museo Civico, Udine. *Signed and dated 1576.*

885. FLORIGERIO: *Madonna in Glory, with Baptist and George killing the Dragon below.*
S. Giorgio, Udine. *1529-30.*

886. FLORIGERIO: *Anne and Madonna enthroned between Roch and Sebastian; Lunette with John the Evangelist between Francis and Anthony of Padua (detail)*. Accademia, Venice.

887. FLORIGERIO: *Half-length portrait of Man*. Uffizi, Florence.

888. UNIDENTIFIED FOLLOWER OF PORDENONE: *Dead Christ upheld by Putti*. Monte di Pietà, Treviso.

897. GIROLAMO DI TOMMASO DA TREVISO: *Monochrome fresco: Miracle of Anthony of Padua: the speech of the new-born Baby.* S. Petronio, Bologna. *Signed and dated 1525.*

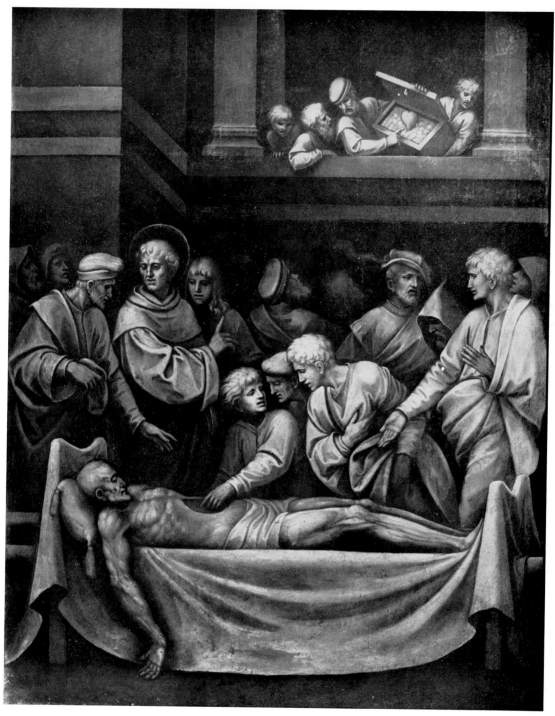

898. Girolamo di Tommaso da Treviso: *Monochrome fresco: Miracle of Anthony of Padua: the heart of the Miser.* S. Petronio, Bologna. *Signed and dated 1525.*

902. (?) DOMENICO CAPRIOLI: *Pilgrim and Lovers in landscape.* Mr. Guy Benson, London.

903. Domenico Caprioli: *Adoration of the Shepherds*. Museo Civico, Treviso. *Signed and dated 1518.*

905. DOMENICO CAPRIOLI: *Portrait of Lelio Torelli.*
Bowes Museum, Barnard Castle. *Signed and dated 1528.*

904. DOMENICO CAPRIOLI: *Portrait of Youth.*
Duke of Grafton, London. *Signed and dated 1512.*

907. ROCCO MARCONI: *Bust of Christ blessing. Formerly Dr. J. S. Maynard, London.*

906. ROCCO MARCONI: *Copy of Northbrook Bellini Madonna. Schlesisches Museum, Breslau. Signature painted over to read 'Opus Joannes Bellini'.*

908. ROCCO MARCONI: *Christ with Mary and Martha*. County Museum, Los Angeles (California).

909. ROCCO MARCONI: *Christ and the Adulteress. Accademia, Venice. Signed.*

910. PALMA VECCHIO AND CATENA: *Christ and the Samaritan Woman at the Well.*
Formerly Charles Butler, London.

911. PALMA VECCHIO: *Madonna with Francis, Jerome and female Donor.* Galleria Borghese, Rome.
Before 1500.

912. PALMA VECCHIO: *Venus and Mars*. Brooklyn Museum, New York.

913. PALMA VECCHIO: *Youth with pipes and Maiden singing* (*fragment*). Mrs. W. M. H. Pollen, Norton Hall (Glos.).
914. PALMA VECCHIO: *Open-air Concert.* Lady Colum Crichton-Stuart, Ardencraig (Rothesay, Scotland).

914

913

915. PALMA VECCHIO: *Halberdier watching Woman seated in meadow and two Infants (Mars, Rhea Sylvia, Romulus and Remus?)*. Wilstach Collection, Philadelphia (Pa.).

916. PALMA VECCHIO: *Adam and Eve*. Landesmuseum, Brunswick.

917. PALMA VECCHIO: *Madonna with George, Lucy and music-making Angel.* S. Stefano, Vicenza.

919. PALMA VECCHIO: *Young Woman meditating and holding lute.*
Duke of Northumberland, Alnwick Castle (Northd.).

918. PALMA VECCHIO: *Young Man holding glove.*
Hermitage, Leningrad.

921. PALMA VECCHIO: *'Violante'*. Kunsthistorisches Museum, Vienna.

920. PALMA VECCHIO: *A Poet*. National Gallery, London.

922. PALMA VECCHIO: *Adoration of the Shepherds with female Donor.* Louvre, Paris.

923. PALMA VECCHIO: *Sacra Conversazione with Baptist, female Martyr and Peter.*
Corporation Art Gallery, Glasgow.

924. PALMA VECCHIO: *Sacra Conversazione with Michael, Dorothea, Magdalen and (?) Mark.*
National Gallery, Prague.

925. PALMA VECCHIO (FINISHED BY TITIAN): *Sacra Conversazione with Baptist, Magdalen and Joseph.*
Accademia, Venice.

926. PALMA VECCHIO: *Venus and Cupid in landscape*. Fitzwilliam Museum, Cambridge.

927. PALMA VECCHIO: *Diana and Callisto*. Kunsthistorisches Museum, Vienna.

928. PALMA VECCHIO: *Half-length portrait of Paola Priuli, wife of Francesco Querini (unfinished)*.
Pinacoteca Querini Stampalia, Venice.

929. PALMA VECCHIO: *Sketch of bearded Man (Self-portrait?) on back of female Portrait.*
Contini Bonacossi Collection, Florence.

930. FRANCESCO VECELLIO: *Madonna against curtain*. Homeless.

931. FRANCESCO VECELLIO: *Sebastian and Infant Baptist* (*fragment of a 'Sacra Conversazione'*). Homeless.

932. Francesco Vecellio: *Madonna with Roch and Sebastian.* Formerly Holford Collection, London.

934. FRANCESCO VECELLIO: *Version of Giorgione's 'Allendale Nativity'*
(finished by Titian). S. H. Kress Collection,
Museum of Fine Arts, Houston (Texas). *ca 1525.*

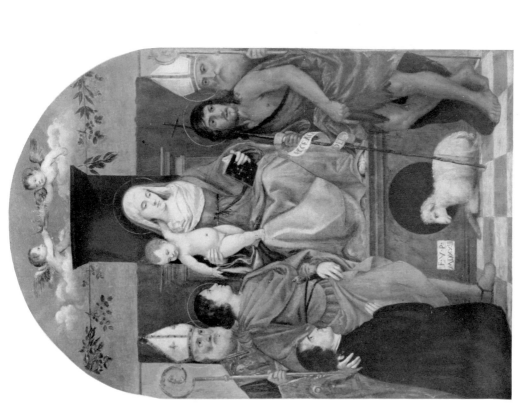

933. FRANCESCO VECELLIO: *Madonna with Gothard, Modestus,*
Baptist, Vitus and the kneeling Bernardo Costantini.
Chiesa Pievanale, San Vito di Cadore. *Signed and dated 1524.*

936. Francesco Vecellio: *Bust of Youth with large hat.*
Kunsthistorisches Museum, Vienna.

935. Francesco Vecellio: *Bust of cleanshaven Man.*
Homeless.

937. Francesco Vecellio: *Mystical Marriage of Catherine*. Formerly Cook Collection, Richmond (Surrey).

938. Francesco Vecellio: *Organ-shutter: Resurrection*. S. Salvatore, Venice. *1530-35*.

939. FRANCESCO VECELLIO: *Organ-shutter: Theodore*. S. Salvatore, Venice. *1530-35*.

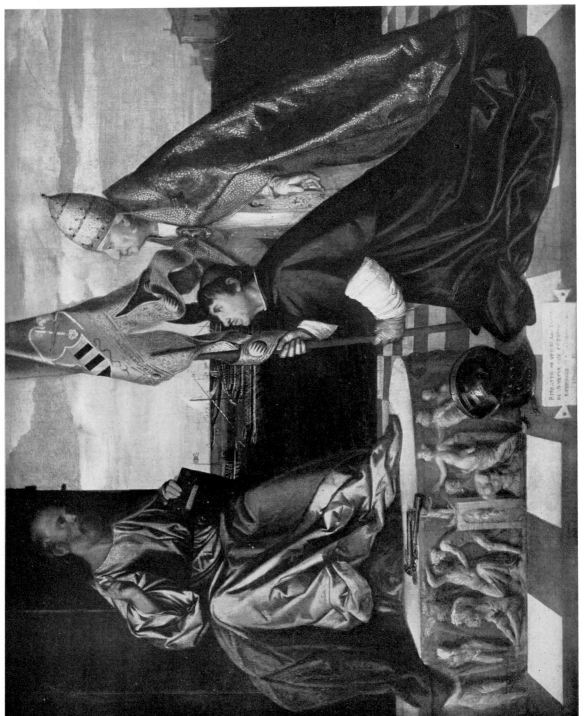

216 TITIAN: Pope Alexander VI presenting Doge Bello to Peter. Musée Royal des Beaux-Arts, Antwerp.

941. TITIAN: *Fresco: The speech of the new-born Child.* Scuola del Santo, Padua. *1511.*

942. TITIAN: *Detail from Plate 941.*

943. TITIAN: *Christ and the Adulteress (unfinished)*. Kunsthistorisches Museum, Vienna.

944. TITIAN: *Male portrait*. National Gallery, London. *Signed*.

945. TITIAN: '*La Schiavona*'. National Gallery, London.

958. Titian: *Bacchanal*. Prado, Madrid. *Signed*. *1516-18*.

959. TITIAN: *Detail from the Worship of Venus*. Prado, Madrid. *1516-18*.

960. TITIAN: *Sacra Conversazione with Dominic, Catherine and Donor. Doria-Balbi Collection, Genoa.   ca 1515.*

962. TITIAN: *Young Man holding his cap.*
Earl of Halifax, Garrowby Hall (Yorks.). *ca 1520.*

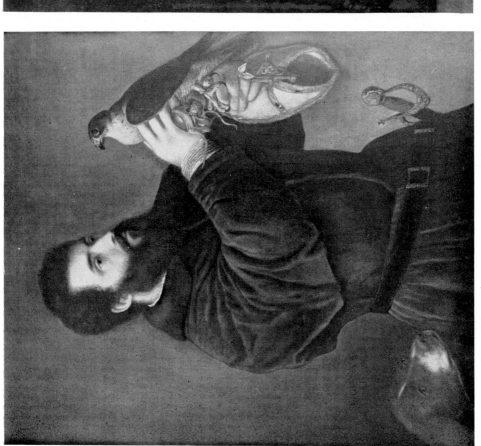

961. TITIAN: *Gentleman with Hawk and Hound.*
Jocelyn Memorial Art Gallery, Omaha (Nebraska). *Signed. ca 1525.*

963. TITIAN: *Endymion and his flock (furniture painting, detail)*. Barnes Foundation, Merion (Pa.).

964. TITIAN: *Supper at Emmaus*. Earl of Yarborough, Brocklesby Park (Lincs.). *Signed.*

965. TITIAN: *Nazarus, Celsus and the papal Legate Altobello Averoldo*
(detail from Polyptych of Resurrection.)
SS. Nazzaro e Celso, Brescia. *Signed and dated 1522.*

966. TITIAN: *Resurrection (centre of polyptych)*. SS. Nazzaro e Celso,
Brescia. *Signed and dated 1522.*

967. TITIAN: *Madonna appearing to Francis, Aloysius and Donor (from S. Francesco).* Pinacoteca, Ancona.
Signed and dated *1520*.

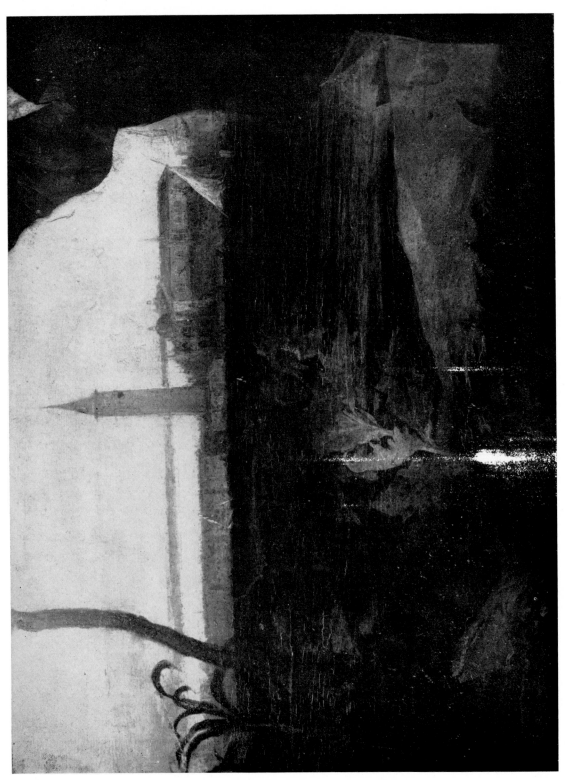

268 · TITIAN · Detail from Plate 267

969. TITIAN: *Entombment.* Louvre, Paris. *ca 1526.*

970. TITIAN: *Lady with young Moor (called 'Laura de' Dianti')*. Formerly Cook Collection, Richmond (Surrey). *ca 1523*.

971. TITIAN: *Venus rising from the sea*. Earl of Ellesmere Loan, National Gallery of Scotland, Edinburgh.

972. TITIAN: 'La Vierge au lapin'. Louvre, Paris. Signed. (?) 1530.

973. TITIAN: *Jerome in the Wilderness*. Louvre, Paris.

975. TITIAN: *Charles V with dog.* Prado, Madrid.
1533.

974. TITIAN: *Cardinal Ippolito de' Medici in Hungarian costume.*
Uffizi, Florence. 1533.

976. Titian: *Presentation of the Virgin.* Accademia, Venice. *1538.*

977. TITIAN: *Detail from Plate 976.*

978. TITIAN: *Portrait of Lady known as 'La Bella'*. Pitti, Florence. *ca 1536.*

980. TITIAN: *Girl in fur, with plumed hat.* Hermitage, Leningrad.

979. TITIAN: *Girl in fur.* Kunsthistorisches Museum, Vienna.

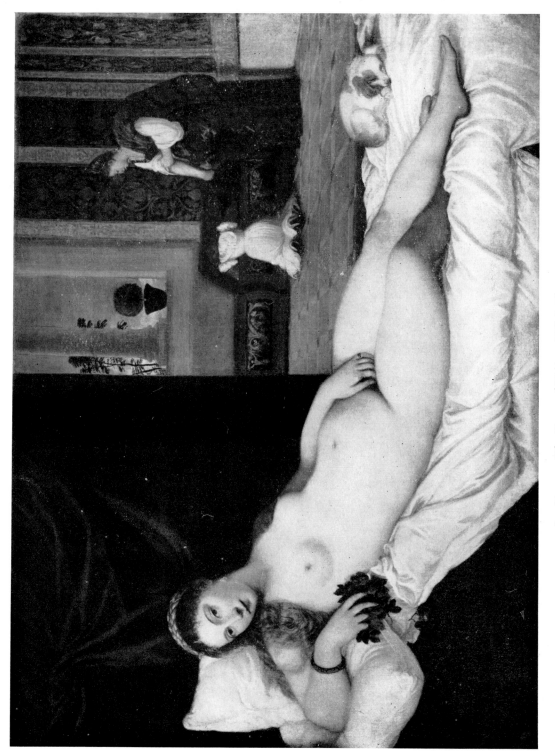

981. TITIAN: *The Venus of Urbino*. Uffizi, Florence, *1538*.

982. TITIAN: *Doge Andrea Gritti (1454–1538).* S. H. Kress Foundation,
New York. *Signed.*

983. TITIAN: *Pietro Aretino.* Pitti, Florence. *Not later than 1545.*

985. TITIAN: *Pier Luigi Farnese with a Standard-bearer.*
Museo Nazionale, Naples. 1546.

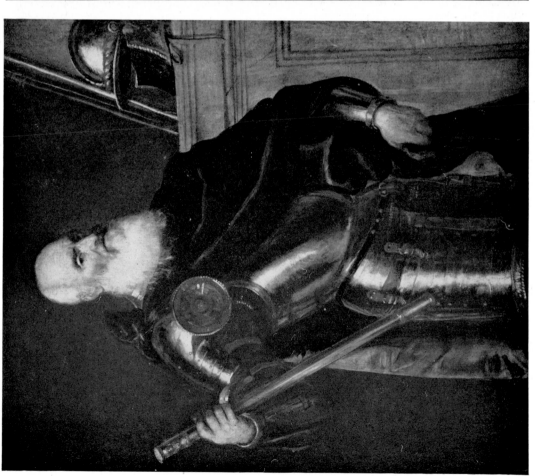

984. TITIAN: *Admiral Vincenzo Cappello* (?1541). S. H. Kress Foundation,
New York.

989. TITIAN: *Pope Paul III*. Museo Nazionale, Naples. *1543*.

990. TITIAN: *Pope Paul III with Alessandro and Ottavio Farnese (unfinished)*. Museo Nazionale, Naples. *1546*.

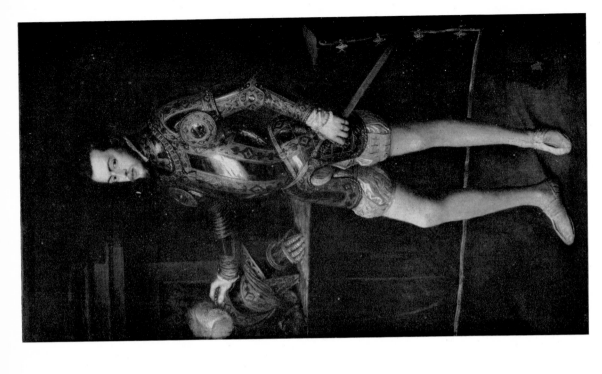

992. TITIAN: *Philip II in armour*. Prado, Madrid. *1550*.

991. TITIAN: *Don Diego de Mendoza*. Pitti, Florence.

994. TITIAN: *Philip II with crown and sceptre (unfinished)*.
Art Museum, Cincinnati (Ohio). ca 1555.

993. TITIAN: *Self-portrait*. Staatliche Museen, Berlin.

995. TITIAN: *Danaë. Prado, Madrid. Not later than 1553.*

996. TITIAN: *Perseus and Andromeda*. Wallace Collection, London.

997. TITIAN: *Venus and Adonis*. Metropolitan Museum of Art, New York. 1550-55.

998. TITIAN: *Entombment, with Self-portrait as Joseph of Arimathea. Prado, Madrid. Signed and dated 1559.*

999. TITIAN: *Diana and Actaeon*. Earl of Ellesmere Loan, National Gallery of Scotland, Edinburgh.
Signed. 1559.

1000. TITIAN: *Diana and Actaeon*. Earl of Harewood, Harewood House (Yorks.).

1004. TITIAN AND ASSISTANTS: *The Magdalen with Blaise, Tobias, the Angel and Donor.* S. Domenico, Dubrovnik.

1003. TITIAN: *The penitent Magdalen.* Hermitage, Leningrad. *Signed.*

1006. TITIAN: *Madonna.* Albertini Collection, Rome.

1005. TITIAN: *Madonna.* Alte Pinakothek, Munich. *Signed.*

1008. TITIAN: *Self-portrait with drawing block*. Formerly Lord Ashburnham, Ashburnham Place (Sussex). *ca 1560*.

1007. TITIAN: *The Marquess of Savignano*. Bankes Collection, Kingston Lacy (Wimborne, Dorset). *ca 1550*.

1009. TITIAN: *Venus with Luteplayer.* Metropolitan Museum of Art, New York. *1560–65.*

1010. TITIAN: *Portrait of (?)Muhrad III*. Italico Brass Collection, Venice.

1011. TITIAN: *Jacopo da Strada.* Kunsthistorisches Museum, Vienna. *Signed and dated 1566.*

1013. TITIAN: *Christ on the Cross with Mary, John and Dominic. S. Domenico, Ancona. Signed. Before 1567.*

1012. TITIAN: *Christ on the Cross. Sacristy, Escorial.*

1015. TITIAN: *Margaret and the Dragon.* Prado, Madrid. *Signed. ca 1565.*

1014. TITIAN: *Catherine adoring the Crucifix.* Museum of Fine Arts, Boston.

1016. TITIAN: *Martyrdom of Lawrence*. Iglesia Vieja, Escorial. *1567*.

1017. TITIAN: *The Flaying of Marsyas*. Archiepiscopal Gallery, Kremsier.

1019. TITIAN: *Detail from Plate 1017.*

1018. TITIAN: *Annunciation. S. Salvatore, Venice.*
Signed twice.

1020. TITIAN: *Putto with Dogs (fragment).* Van Beuningen Collection, Vierhouten (Otterlo).

1021. TITIAN: *Madonna with Saints Titian and Andrew, and Titian himself as Donor.* Chiesa Arcidiaconale, Pieve di Cadore.

1022. TITIAN: *Pietà. Accademia, Venice. Begun in 1573, finished by Palma Giovane.*

1025. DOMENICO CAMPAGNOLA: *Anthony of Padua resuscitating a drowned Girl*. Scuola del Santo, Padua.

1026. DOMENICO CAMPAGNOLA: *Madonna with George and Catherine of Alexandria.*
J. G. Johnson Collection, Philadelphia (Pa.).

1027. DOMENICO CAMPAGNOLA: *Holy Family and three Saints.* Conte Novello Papafava, Padua.

1028. DOMENICO CAMPAGNOLA: *Madonna enthroned between Lucas and Mark, and Baptism of Justina (from the Palazzo del Podestà).* Museo Civico, Padua. 1537.

1029. Domenico Campagnola: *The Good Samaritan.* S. H. Kress Foundation, New York. *Late work.*

1030. POLIDORO DA LANCIANO: *Madonna in landscape, worshipped by two Angels.*
Formerly Lederer Collection Vienna.

1031. POLIDORO DA LANCIANO: *Holy Family in landscape, with two kneeling Donors.*
Formerly Frank and Henry Farrer, London.

1032. POLIDORO DA LANCIANO: *Sacra Conversazione with Infant Baptist, Catherine and Joseph.*
Formerly Lord Melchett, London.

1033. POLIDORO DA LANCIANO: *Holy Family with the Magdalen, a Venetian Nobleman and his Child.*
Gemäldegalerie, Dresden.

1034. PAOLO VERONESE: *The 'Bevilacqua' Altarpiece*. Museo di Castelvecchio, Verona. *1548*.

The inscription on the pedestal reads:

DATVM EST
DESVPER

FRANCISCVS
FRANCESCHINV
ANNÆ · XXVIII
M · D · L I ·

1035. PAOLO VERONESE: *Portrait of Francesco Franceschini*. Ringling Museum, Sarasota (Florida).
Dated 1551.

1036. PAOLO VERONESE: *Detached fresco from the villa Soranza: Temperance.*
Sacristy, S. Liberale, Castelfranco Veneto. *1551.*

1037. PAOLO VERONESE: *Holy Family with George and Infant Baptist*. Ashmolean Museum, Oxford.

1038. PAOLO VERONESE: *Martyrdom of Justina*. Uffizi, Florence.

1039. PAOLO VERONESE: *Epiphany*. Col. F. J. Davies, London.

1040. PAOLO VERONESE: *Supper at Emmaus.* Louvre, Paris. *Signed.*

1041. PAOLO VERONESE: *Portrait of Pase Guarienti*. Museo di Castelvecchio, Verona. *Dated 1556.*

1042. PAOLO VERONESE: *Portrait of Gentleman*. Formerly Conte Salvi Pindemonte Moscardo, Verona.

1043. PAOLO VERONESE: *Young Man between Learning and Pleasure*. National Gallery of Victoria, Melbourne.

1044. PAOLO VERONESE: *Ceiling: Triumph of Mordecai*.
S. Sebastiano, Venice. *1556*.

1045. Paolo Veronese: *Organ-shutters (outside): Purification of the Virgin; on parapet, Nativity and two Allegorical Figures.* S. Sebastiano, Venice. *1559-60.*

1046. Paolo Veronese: *Martyrdom of George*. S. Giorgio in Braida, Verona.

1047. PAOLO VERONESE: *Ceiling Fresco: Olympus or the Planetary System*. Villa Barbaro, Maser (Treviso). *ca 1561*.

1048. PAOLO VERONESE: *Ceiling Fresco: Fortitude, Abundance and Envy*. Villa Barbaro, Maser (Treviso). *ca 1561*

1049. PAOLO VERONESE: *Fresco: Lunette with Summer and Autumn between Cybele (Earth) and Neptune (Water)*.
Villa Barbaro, Maser (Treviso).

1050. PAOLO VERONESE: *Frescoes at juncture of passages: Allegorical Figures, Landscapes, a Servant*.
Villa Barbaro, Maser. (Treviso)

1051. Paolo Veronese: *Fresco: Lunette with Winter and Spring between Juno (Air) and Vulcan (Fire)*. Villa Barbaro, Maser (Treviso).

1052. Paolo Veronese: *Fresco decoration of wall*. Villa Barbaro, Maser (Treviso).

1053. PAOLO VERONESE: *Fresco decoration of a small room:*
'Madonna della Pappa', View of a Harbour, Statues and Grotesques. Villa Barbaro, Maser (Treviso). *ca 1561.*

1061. PAOLO VERONESE: *Detail from Plate 1060.*

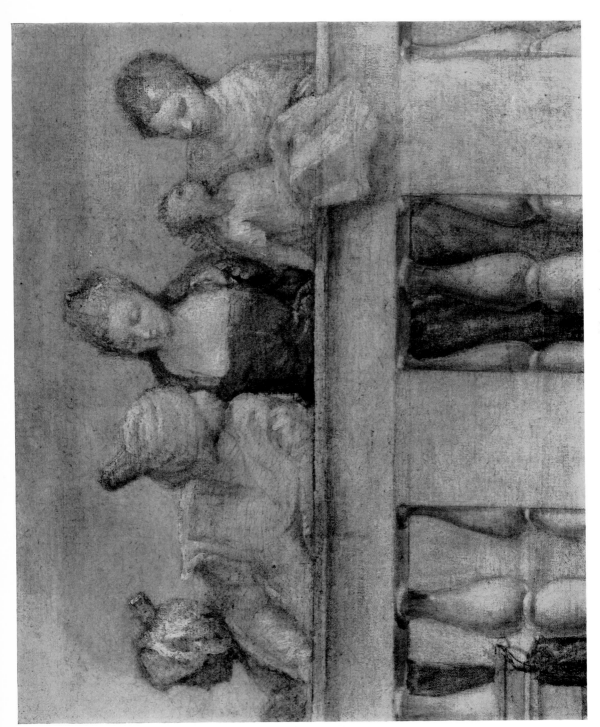

1062. PAOLO VERONESE: *Detail from Plate 1060.*

1063. PAOLO VERONESE: *The Marriage at Cana (from S. Giorgio Maggiore, Venice). (Detail).* Louvre, Paris. 1563.

1064. PAOLO VERONESE: *Portrait of a Lady*. Musée, Douai.

1065. PAOLO VERONESE: *Marriage of Catherine*. Royal Collections, Hampton Court.
Reproduced by gracious permission of H.M. the Queen

1066. Paolo Veronese: *Antonio and Giambattista Marogna being commended to the Virgin by their eponymous Saints, Anthony of Padua and John the Baptist.* S. Paolo, Verona. *Not before 1565.*

1067. PAOLO VERONESE: Ceiling: *Annunciation (from S. Maria dell'Umiltà)*. Cappella del Rosario, SS. Giovanni e Paolo, Venice. *Before 1568*.

1068. Paolo Veronese: *Christ among the Doctors. Prado, Madrid. ca 1565.*

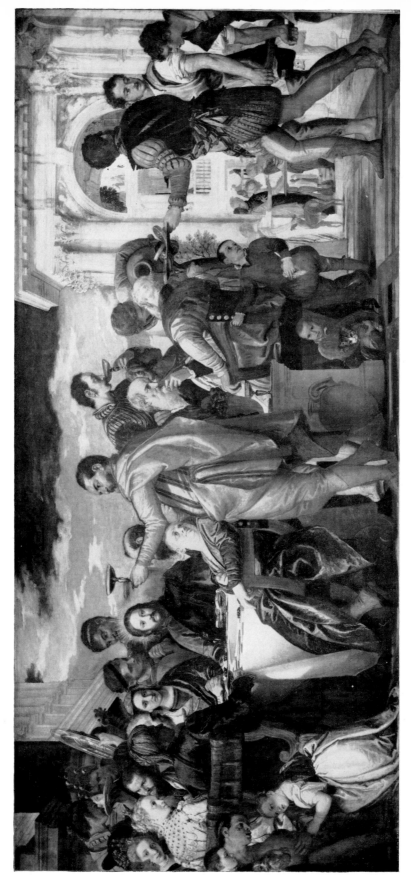

1069. PAOLO VERONESE: *The Marriage at Cana (from the Palazzo Cuccina)*. Gemäldegalerie, Dresden.

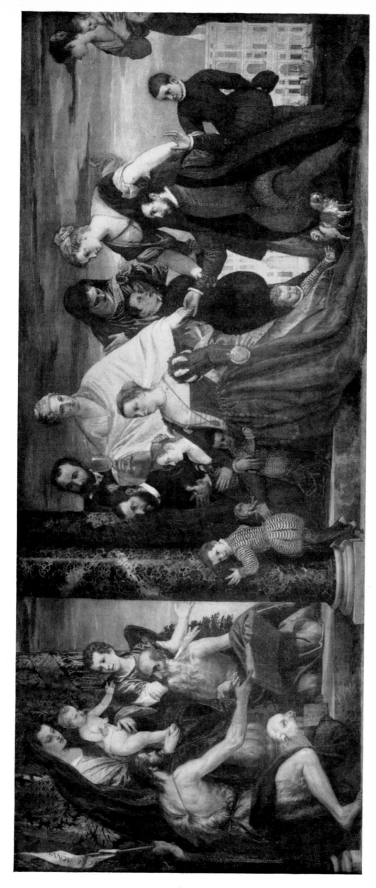

1070. PAOLO VERONESE: *The Cuccina Family commended to the Virgin, the Baptist and Jerome, by Faith, Charity and Hope.* Gemäldegalerie, Dresden.

1071. PAOLO VERONESE: *Detail from Plate 1072.*

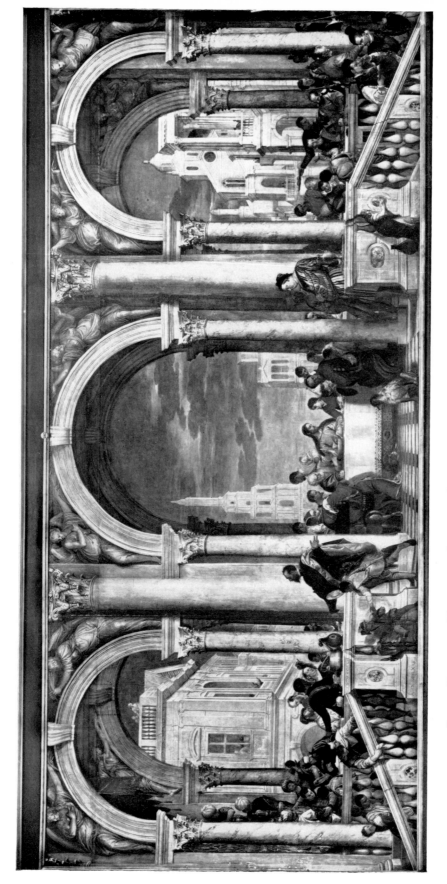

1072. PAOLO VERONESE: *The Feast in the House of Levi (from SS. Giovanni e Paolo). Accademia, Venice. Dated 1573.*

1073. PAOLO VERONESE: *Allegory of the Battle of Lepanto, with Venice in a white cloak, commended to the Virgin by Peter, James, Justina and Mark*. Accademia, Venice. *1571*.

1074. Paolo Veronese: *Epiphany*. S. Corona, Vicenza. *Not before 1573*.

1075–76. PAOLO VERONESE: *Rest on the Flight; Deposition* (*monochromes from the organ parapet in S. Antonio, Torcello*). Musco Provinciale Torcello (Venice.). *1570–75.*

1077. PAOLO VERONESE: *Annunciation*. Museum of Art, Cleveland (Ohio). *1570–75*.

1078. Paolo Veronese: *Meekness*. Dr. Emmons, Hamble (Hampshire).

1079. Paolo Veronese: *Susanna and the Elders*. Ambrogio Doria Collection, Genoa.

1080. Paolo Veronese: *Portrait of a Girl aged 17, destined to become a Nun*. Homeless. Dated 1574.

1081. Paolo Veronese: *Diana and Actaeon*. J. G. Johnson Collection, Philadelphia (Pa.).

1083. PAOLO VERONESE: *Portrait of Daniele Barbaro.*
Gemäldegalerie, Dresden.

1082. PAOLO VERONESE: *Portrait of Alessandro Vittoria.*
Metropolitan Museum of Art, New York.

1084. PAOLO VERONESE: *Cartoon for tapestry: Peter of Amiens exhorts Doge Michele Vital to help the Crusaders. Istituto d'Arte Passaglia, Lucca. 1576–77.*

1085. PAOLO VERONESE: *Venus and Adonis*. Prado, Madrid.

1086. PAOLO VERONESE: *Meekness (detail)*. Ceiling, Sala del Collegio, Palazzo Ducale, Venice. *1575–77*.

1087. PAOLO VERONESE: *The Rape of Europa (detail)*. Rasini Collection, Milan.

1088. PAOLO VERONESE: *The Rape of Europa (detail)*. Sala dell'Anticollegio, Palazzo Ducale, Venice. *1575–80.*

1089. Paolo Veronese: *The Finding of Moses* (*detail*). Prado, Madrid.

1090. PAOLO VERONESE: *Venus and Mars united by Love*. Metropolitan Museum of Art, New York. Signed. 1576–84.

1091. Paolo Veronese: *The Poet between Virtue and Vice*. Copyright The Frick Collection, New York. *1576–84*.

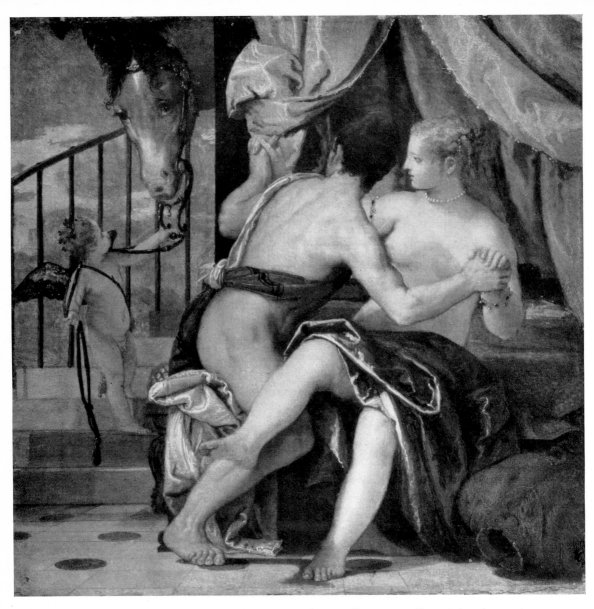

1092. Paolo Veronese: *Venus and Mars*. Gualino Collection, Galleria Sabauda, Turin.

1093. PAOLO VERONESE: *Rest on the Flight*. Ringling Museum, Sarasota (Florida).

1094. PAOLO VERONESE: *The Creation of Eve*. Art Institute, Chicago (Illinois).

1095. Paolo Veronese: *Baptism of Christ*. Lee of Fareham Collection, University, London.

1096. PAOLO VERONESE: *Venus and Adonis*. Kunsthistorisches Museum, Vienna.

1097. PAOLO VERONESE: *David and Batsheba*. Musée, Lyons.

1098. PAOLO VERONESE: *Rebecca at the Well*. National Gallery of Art, Washington.

1099. Paolo Veronese: *Lucretia*. Kunsthistorisches Museum, Vienna.

1100. Paolo Veronese: *Hagar and Ishmael in the Desert*. Kunsthistorisches Museum, Vienna.

1101. Paolo Veronese: *Christ in the Garden*. Brera, Milan.

1102. PAOLO VERONESE: *Pantaleone healing a sick Boy*. S. Pantaleone, Venice. *1587*.

1104. BATTISTA ZELOTTI: *Learning and Pleasure.*
Ceiling, Libreria di S. Marco, Venice. 1557.

1103. BATTISTA ZELOTTI: *Venice and the Lion of St. Mark.*
Ceiling, Sala dei Dieci, Palazzo Ducale, Venice. 1553–54.

1105. BATTISTA ZELOTTI: *Fresco: Story of Sophonisba and Massinissa*. Castello Colleoni, Thiene (Vicenza).

1106. BATTISTA ZELOTTI: *Fresco: Hercules and Dejanira and the dying Centaur*. Villa Emo, Fanzolo (Treviso). *1567–70*.

1107. Battista Zelotti: *Fresco: Allegory of Painting*. Villa Emo, Fanzolo (Treviso). *1567–70*.

1108. BATTISTA ZELOTTI: *Fresco: Decorative Figure (Cleopatra)*. Castello del Cattajo (Padua). *ca 1570*.

1110. FRANCESCO MONTEMEZZANO: *Lady with a Squirrel.*
Rijksmuseum, Amsterdam,

1109. FRANCESCO MONTEMEZZANO: *Portrait of a seated Lady.*
Homeless.

1114. FRANCESCO MONTEMEZZANO: *Baptism.*
Santuario della Madonna, Lendinara (Rovigo).

1113. FRANCESCO MONTEMEZZANO: *Mourning at the Foot of the Cross.*
Formerly Severino Spinelli, Florence.

1116

1115. GIAN PIETRO SILVIO: *Vendemianus between Jerome and Liberale, with dead Christ upheld by Angels above.*
Chiesa Parrocchiale, San Vendemiano (Treviso). *Signed and dated 1549.*
1116. GIAN PIETRO SILVIO: *Dead Christ upheld by Angels. S. Giacomo, Sedrina (Bergamo). Signed.*

1115

1117. PARIS BORDONE: *Six Youths and a Girl in Woods (Cephalus and Procris?), with heraldic Lion and Gryphon in foreground.* Homeless.

1118. PARIS BORDONE: *Sacra Conversazione with Jerome and Anthony Abbot commending a Donor.* Corporation Art Gallery, Glasgow. *Signed.*

1119. PARIS BORDONE: *Christ anointing a Doge in prison*. National Gallery, London.

1120. PARIS BORDONE: *Sacra Conversazione with Baptist, Magdalen and Liberale*.
Corporation Art Gallery, Glasgow.

1121. PARIS BORDONE: *Portrait of a Gentleman aged 30.*
Balbi di Piovera Collection, Genoa. *Dated 1537.*

1122. PARIS BORDONE: *Portrait of a Lady of the Fugger Family.*
Formerly Earl of Rosebery, Mentmore (Bucks.). *ca 1540.*

1123. PARIS BORDONE: *Family Group*. Devonshire Collection, Chatsworth (Derby).

1124. PARIS BORDONE: *George killing the Dragon*. Pinacoteca Vaticana, Rome.

1125. PARIS BORDONE: *The 'Giovannelli' Sacra Conversazione with Jerome and Francis.*
County Museum, Los Angeles (California). *Signed.*

1126. PARIS BORDONE: *Marriage of Catherine, with Infant Baptist.* Balbi di Piovera Collection, Genoa.

1127. PARIS BORDONE: *The Death of Adonis.* Homeless.

1128. PARIS BORDONE: *Parnassus.* Formerly Mr. W. H. Woodward, London.

1129. PARIS BORDONE: *Christ among the Doctors*. Gardner Museum, Boston (Mass.).

1131. Paris Bordone: *Christ blessing.* National Gallery, London. *Signed.*

1130. Paris Bordone: *Apollo between Midas and Marsyas.* Gemäldegalerie, Dresden.

1132. PARIS BORDONE: *Diana as Huntress with two Nymphs* (destroyed in 1945). Gemäldegalerie, Dresden.

1133. PARIS BORDONE: *Abduction of a Nymph*. Homeless. *Signed*.

1134. PARIS BORDONE: *Venus with Flora, Cupid and Mars*. Hermitage, Leningrad.

1135. PARIS BORDONE: *Rest on the Flight, with penitent Jerome*. Homeless.

1136. Paris Bordone: *Batsheba*. Wallraf-Richartz Museum, Cologne. *Signed*.

1137. BONIFAZIO VERONESE: *Sacra Conversazione with Elizabeth, Infant Baptist and Donor offering a Globe to Jesus*. Pitti, Florence.

1138. BONIFAZIO VERONESE: *The Triumph of Love*. Kunsthistorisches Museum, Vienna.

1139. BONIFAZIO VERONESE: *Sacra Conversazione*. Marquess of Lansdowne, Bowood (Calne, Wiltshire).

1140. BONIFAZIO VERONESE: *Lot and his Daughters*. Mr. W. P. Chrysler Jr., New York.

1141. BONIFAZIO VERONESE: *Epiphany.* The Bob Jones University Gallery, Greenville (South Carolina).

1142. BONIFAZIO VERONESE: *Rest on the Flight with Monk behind hedge.* National Gallery of South Australia, Adelaide.

1143. Bonifazio Veronese: *Diana and Callisto*. Dr. W. Suida, New York.

1144. BONIFAZIO VERONESE: *The Finding of Moses.* Brera, Milan.

1145. Bonifazio Veronese: *Mucius Scaevola burning his hand before Porsenna*. Mrs. Julius Weitzner, New York.

1146. Bonifazio Veronese: *The Return of the Prodigal Son.* Galleria Borghese, Rome.

1147–1148. Bonifazio Veronese and Assistants: *Spring; Winter.*
Museum, Budapest.

1149. BONIFAZIO VERONESE: *Christ among the Doctors*. Pitti, Florence.

1150–1151. Workshop of Bonifazio Veronese: *Regulus before the Roman Senate; Archimedes at the Siege of Syracuse; Allegorical and Mythological Figures.* Homeless.

1152. ANDREA SCHIAVONE: *Moses striking Water from the Rock*. Earl of Wemyss, Gosford House (Haddington, Scotland).

1153. ANDREA SCHIAVONE: *Judgement of Midas*. Formerly Mr. Charles Loeser, Florence.

1154. ANDREA SCHIAVONE: *Conversion of Paul.* Pinacoteca Querini Stampalia, Venice.

1155. ANDREA SCHIAVONE: *Allegory of Nature*. Accademia, Venice.

1156. ANDREA SCHIAVONE: *Deucalion and Pyrrha.* Accademia, Venice.

1157. ANDREA SCHIAVONE: *Venus carried by a dolphin to Cythera.* Castello Sforzesco, Milan.

1158. Andrea Schiavone: *Epiphany*. Ambrosiana, Milan.

1159. ANDREA SCHIAVONE: *Departure of Briseis (detail)*. Royal Collections, Hampton Court.
Reproduced by gracious permission of H.M. the Queen

1161. ANDREA SCHIAVONE: *Apollo and a Nymph*.
National Gallery, London.

1160. ANDREA SCHIAVONE: *Apollo and Daphne (detail)*. Formerly Mather Collection,
Princeton (New Jersey).

1162. ANDREA SCHIAVONE: *Marriage of Cupid and Psyche*. Devonshire Collection, Chatsworth.

1163. ANDREA SCHIAVONE: *'Donà delle Rose' Mourning over the dead Christ.*
A. Coin, Venice.

1164. ANDREA SCHIAVONE: *Woman carrying an amphora followed by Prisoner, Horseman and Camels.*
Prince Paul of Yugoslavia, Pratolino, Florence.

1165. ANDREA SCHIAVONE: *Sacra Conversazione*. British Embassy, Rome.

1166. Andrea Schiavone: *Figures in Landscape (detail)*. Royal Collections, Hampton Court.
Reproduced by gracious permission of H.M. the Queen

1167. Andrea Schiavone: *Meeting of Jacob and Rachel (detail)*. Royal Collections, Hampton Court.
Reproduced by gracious permission of H.M. the Queen

1168. Andrea Schiavone: *Blessing of Jacob (detail)*. Royal Collections, Hampton Court.
Reproduced by gracious permission of H.M. the Queen

1168A. *Detail from Plate 1168.*

1169. ANDREA SCHIAVONE: *Christ in the House of Jairus*. Walter P. Chrysler Jr. Collection, New York.

1170. ANDREA SCHIAVONE: *Judgement of Midas*. Royal Collections, Hampton Court.
Reproduced by gracious permission of H.M. the Queen

1171. ANDREA SCHIAVONE: *Circumcision*. Accademia, Venice.

1172. ANDREA SCHIAVONE (AFTER TITIAN): *Holy Family with Catherine and Infant Baptist*.
Kunsthistorisches Museum, Vienna.

1173. ANDREA SCHIAVONE: *Adoration of the Shepherds*. Kunsthistorisches Museum, Vienna.

1174. ANDREA SCHIAVONE: *Bacchus and the Nymphs*. Italico Brass Collection, Venice.

1175. ANDREA SCHIAVONE: *Parapet of organ-loft: Adoration of the Shepherds (detail)*. S. Maria del Carmelo (I Carmini), Venice.

1176. ANDREA SCHIAVONE: *Parapet of organ-loft: Epiphany.* S. Maria del Carmelo (I Carmini), Venice.

1177. ANDREA SCHIAVONE: *Organ-shutters: Paul and Peter.* S. Pietro, Belluno.

1178. ANDREA SCHIAVONE: *Organ-shutter: Angel of Annunciation*. S. Pietro, Belluno.

1179. ANDREA SCHIAVONE: *Organ-shutter: Virgin of Annunciation*. S. Pietro, Belluno.

1180. ANDREA SCHIAVONE: *Giorgio Cornaro on horseback*. Hon. Mrs. Marten, Crichel (Wimborne, Dorset).

1181. Andrea Schiavone: *Ceiling: The Force of Arms*. Libreria Sansoviniana, Venice. *1556–57*.

1182. ANDREA SCHIAVONE: *A Philosopher*. Libreria Sansoviniana, Venice. 1556–57.

1183. ANDREA SCHIAVONE: *The 'Ellesmere' Christ before Pilate*. Statensmuseum, Stockholm.

1184. ANDREA SCHIAVONE: *The Flight of Aeneas from Troy*. Steirisches Landesmuseum, Graz.

1186. JACOPO BASSANO: *Entombment.*
Chiesa Parrocchiale, San Luca di Crosara (Vicenza).

1185. FRANCESCO BASSANO THE ELDER and his son JACOPO: *Pietà.*
Museo Civico, Bassano del Grappa. *ca 1530.*

1187. JACOPO BASSANO: *Podestà Matteo Soranzo and his Family worshipping the Virgin, Mark, Francis and Lucy.* Museo Civico, Bassano del Grappa. Signed and once dated 1536.

1191. JACOPO BASSANO: *Madonna with Infant Baptist*. Homeless.

1192. JACOPO BASSANO: *Christ on the road to Calvary*. Fitzwilliam Museum, Cambridge.

1193. JACOPO BASSANO: *Adoration of the Shepherds*. Conte J. Giusti del Giardino, Verona.

1194. Jacopo Bassano: *Madonna with James and John the Baptist*. Alte Pinakothek, Munich.

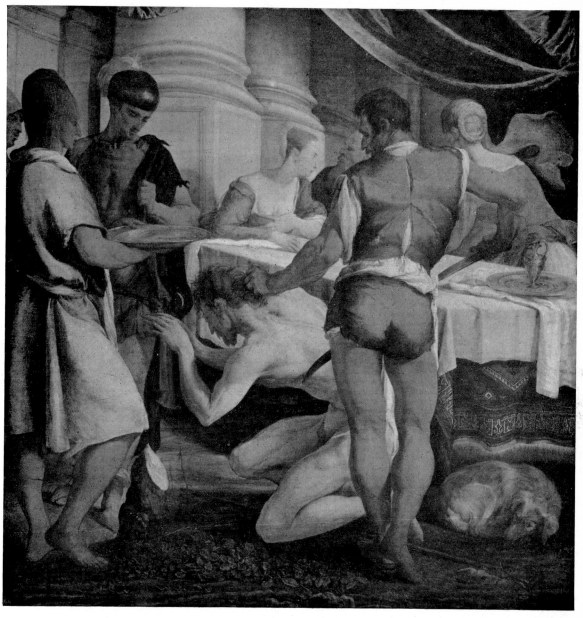

1195. Jacopo Bassano: *Beheading of John the Baptist*. Royal Museum of Fine Arts, Copenhagen. *ca 1555*.

1196. JACOPO BASSANO: *Adoration of the Shepherds*. Galleria Borghese, Rome.

1197. JACOPO BASSANO: *Dives and Lazarus*. Museum of Fine Arts, Cleveland (Ohio).

1198. Jacopo Bassano: *Justina enthroned, with Sebastian, Anthony Abbot and Roch*.
Chiesa Parrocchiale, Enego (Vicenza). *ca 1560*.

1199. JACOPO BASSANO: *The Baptist in the Wilderness*. Museo Civico, Bassano del Grappa

1200. JACOPO BASSANO: *Jerome in the Wilderness*. Fitzwilliam Museum, Cambridge.

1201. JACOPO BASSANO: *Christ on the Cross, with Mary, Magdalen, John the Evangelist and Jerome*
(from S. Teonisto). Museo Civico, Treviso. *1562*.

1202. Jacopo Bassano: 'Il Presepio di S. Giuseppe'. Museo Civico, Bassano del Grappa.
Signed and dated 1568.

1203. GIROLAMO BASSANO: *Version of his father's 'Presepio di S. Giuseppe'.*
Kunsthistorisches Museum, Vienna. *Signed.*

1205. JACOPO BASSANO: *Portrait of an old Woman.*
Mr. O. V. Watney, Cornbury Park, Charlbury (Oxon.).

1204. JACOPO BASSANO: *Portrait of a Painter.*
Uffizi, Florence.

1206. JACOPO BASSANO: *Epiphany*. Kunsthistorisches Museum, Vienna. *1565–70*.

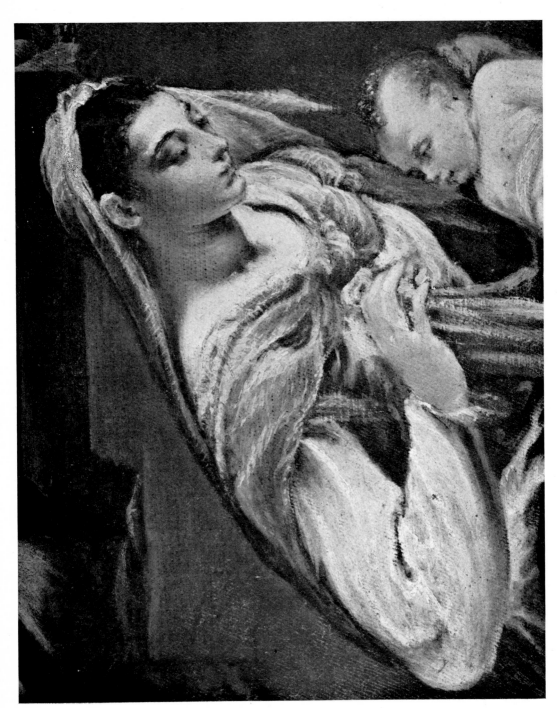

1207. JACOPO BASSANO: *Detail of Plate 1206.*

1208. Jacopo Bassano: *Madonna with Infant Baptist.* Contini Bonacossi Collection, Florence. *Signed. ca 1570.*

1209. Jacopo Bassano: *Adoration of the Shepherds*. Galleria Nazionale (Palazzo Barberini), Rome. *1570-75*.

1210. LEANDRO BASSANO: *Version of Jacopo's Adoration of the Shepherds in the Galleria Nazionale, Rome.*
S. H. Kress Gift to the Fine Arts Club of Arkansas, Little Rock (Arkansas).

1211. JACOPO BASSANO and his son FRANCESCO: Lunette: *The Rettori of Vicenza worshipping the Virgin, Mark and Stephen*. Museo Civico, Vicenza. *Signed. 1573*.

1212. Jacopo Bassano: *Thamar led to the Stake.* Kunsthistorisches Museum, Vienna.

1213. JACOPO BASSANO: *Sketch for the Preaching of Paul*. S. H. Kress Foundation, New York.

1214. JACOPO BASSANO and his son FRANCESCO: *The Preaching of Paul, and John the Evangelist in Glory above.*
S. Antonio, Marostica. *Signed by both painters and dated 1574.*

1215. JACOPO BASSANO: *Eleutherius blessing the Faithful*. Accademia, Venice.

1216. JACOPO BASSANO: *Sketch for an Assumption*. Royal Museum of Fine Arts, Copenhagen.

1217. JACOPO BASSANO: *Sketch for a Birth of the Baptist*. Rhode Island School of Design, Providence (R.I.).

1219. JACOPO BASSANO and his son GIROLAMO: *Madonna in Glory,
with Agatha and Apollonia*. Museo Civico, Bassano del Grappa. *Sd.* 1580–81.

1218. JACOPO BASSANO and his son GIROLAMO: *Martin and the Beggar,
with Anthony Abbot*. Museo Civico, Bassano del Grappa. 1578–80.

1220. GIROLAMO BASSANO: *Shepherds in landscape*. Museum, Budapest.

1221. FRANCESCO BASSANO THE YOUNGER:
Boy playing the flute.
Kunsthistorisches Museum, Vienna. *Signed.*

1222. FRANCESCO BASSANO THE YOUNGER:
Boy with candle.
B. M. and M. L. Greene, Toronto.

1223. FRANCESCO BASSANO THE YOUNGER: *Last Supper*. Prado, Madrid. *Signed.*

1224. Francesco Bassano the Younger: *Pope Alexander III gives Doge Ziani the blessed sword to fight Barbarossa.* Sala del Maggior Consiglio, Palazzo Ducale, Venice.

1225. Francesco Bassano the Younger: *Epiphany*. Kunsthistorisches Museum, Vienna.
Signed. 1575–80.

1226. FRANCESCO BASSANO THE YOUNGER: *Christ in the Garden*.
Ringling Museum, Sarasota (Florida). *Signed.*

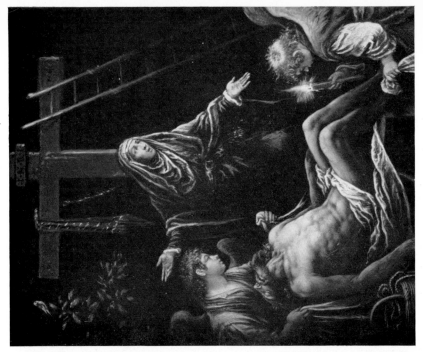

1228. LEANDRO BASSANO: *Pietà*. Palais Attems, Graz.

1227. FRANCESCO BASSANO THE YOUNGER: *Allegory of Water (from a set of the Four Elements)*. Ringling Museum, Sarasota (Florida).

1230. LEANDRO BASSANO: *Luteplayer.*
Formerly Prince Casimir Lubomirski, Cracow. *Signed. 1600.*

1229. LEANDRO BASSANO: *Portrait of old Woman with rosary.*
Earl of Crawford, Balcarres (Fife, Scotland).

1231. LEANDRO BASSANO: *Diana and Actaeon*. Homeless.

1232. LEANDRO BASSANO: *Susanna and the Elders*. Italico Brass Collection, Venice. *Signed*.

1233. LEANDRO BASSANO: *Last Judgement*. S. H. Kress Foundation, New York. *Signed.*

1235. Pietro Mariscalchi (Lo Spada): *Doctor Zaccaria dal Pozzo at the age of 102.* Pinacoteca, Feltre. *1561.*

1234. Pietro Mariscalchi (Lo Spada): *Madonna with Peter and Baptist.* Chiesa Arcipretale, Mel (Belluno). *Signed and dated 155–.*

1237. Pietro Mariscalchi (Lo Spada): *The Baptist between Catherine and Roch.* Chiesa Arcipretale, Sedico (Belluno).

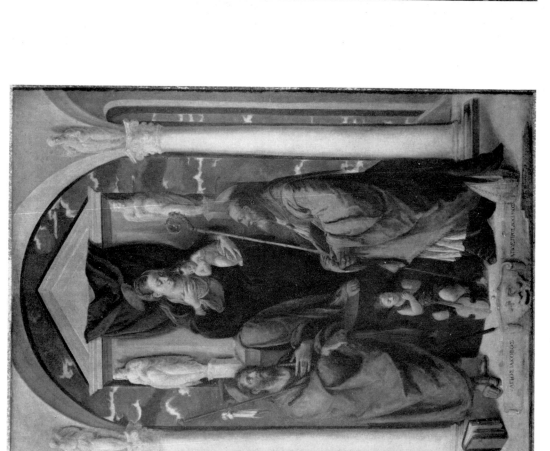

1236. Pietro Mariscalchi (Lo Spada): *Madonna with James, Prosdocimus and Putto with violin.* Walter P. Chrysler Jr. Collection, New York. *Signed and dated 1564.*

1238. PIETRO MARISCALCHI (LO SPADA): *Madonna of Mercy, and sixteen scenes from her Life in predella and above (detail of centre part).* Duomo, Feltre. *Signed.*

1239. PIETRO MARISCALCHI (LO SPADA): *Presentation of the Virgin (detail from the Madonna of Mercy).* Duomo, Feltre. *Signed.*

1240. PIETRO MARISCALCHI (LO SPADA): *Bearded Gentleman with book in right hand.* Homeless.

1241. PIETRO MARISCALCHI (LO SPADA): *Pietà surrounded by the Symbols of the Passion and worshipped by Clare and Scholastica*. S. Maria Assunta e S. Bellino, Bassanello (Padua).

1242. Lambert Sustris: *Reclining Venus*. Rijksmuseum, Amsterdam.

1243. Lambert Sustris: '*Noli me tangere*'. Musée, Lille. *ca 1548*.

1244. LAMBERT SUSTRIS: *Christoph Vöhlin von Frickenhausen*. Alte Pinakothek, Munich.
Dated 1552.

1245. LAMBERT SUSTRIS: *Veronika Vöhlin von Frickenhausen*. Alte Pinakothek, Munich.
Dated 1552.

1246. LAMBERT SUSTRIS: *Diana and Actaeon*. Royal Collections, Hampton Court.
Reproduced by gracious permission of H M. the Queen

1247. LAMBERT SUSTRIS: *The Rape of Proserpina*. Fitzwilliam Museum, Cambridge.

1248. LAMBERT SUSTRIS: *Gentleman with left hand on pommel of sword.* Kunsthistorisches Museum, Vienna.

1249. LAMBERT SUSTRIS: *The Triumph of Fortune.* Formerly Sir Otto Beit, Welwyn (Herts.).

1250. LAMBERT SUSTRIS: *The Triumph of Love.* Prof. R. Longhi, Florence.

1251. LAMBERT SUSTRIS: *Christ on the road to Calvary and Veronica. Brera, Milan. Signed. ca 1560.*

1252. Lambert Sustris: *Venus and Cupid, with Mars in background. Louvre, Paris.*

1256. Giovanni Galizzi: *Madonna*. Agliardi Collection, Bergamo. *Signed and dated 1543.*

1257. GIOVANNI GALIZZI: *Mark between James and Patrick*. Sacristy, S. Maria Assunta, Vertova (Bergamo). Signed and dated 1547.

1258. JACOPO TINTORETTO: *Self-Portrait*. Mr. Max Ascoli, New York. *1545–50.*

IACOBVS·TENTORETVS·PICT·VENT OR· IVS·

·IPSIVS·F·

1259. JACOPO TINTORETTO: *Self-Portrait*. Louvre, Paris. *1588*.

1260. Jacopo Tintoretto: *Sacra Conversazione, with Zacharias, Elizabeth, Infant Baptist, Joseph, Catherine and Francis.* Homeless. *ca 1540.*

1261. Jacopo Tintoretto: *Christ among the Doctors.* Museo del Duomo, Milan. *1542–43.*

1262. JACOPO TINTORETTO: *Supper at Emmaus*. Museum, Budapest.

1263. JACOPO TINTORETTO: *Christ and the Adulteress*. Gemäldegalerie, Dresden.

1264. Jacopo Tintoretto: *Ceiling: The Contest between Apollo and Marsyas.*
Wadsworth Atheneum, Hartford (Connecticut). *1545.*

1265. Jacopo Tintoretto: *The Raising of Lazarus.* Museum der Bildenden Künste, Leipzig.

1266. Jacopo Tintoretto: *Ursula and her Virgins*. S. Lazzaro dei Mendicanti, Venice.

1267. Jacopo Tintoretto: *Solomon and the Queen of Sheba*. Kunsthistorisches Museum, Vienna. *ca. 1545.*

1268. Jacopo Tintoretto: *David bringing the Ark to Jerusalem*. Kunsthistorisches Museum, Vienna. *ca 1548.*

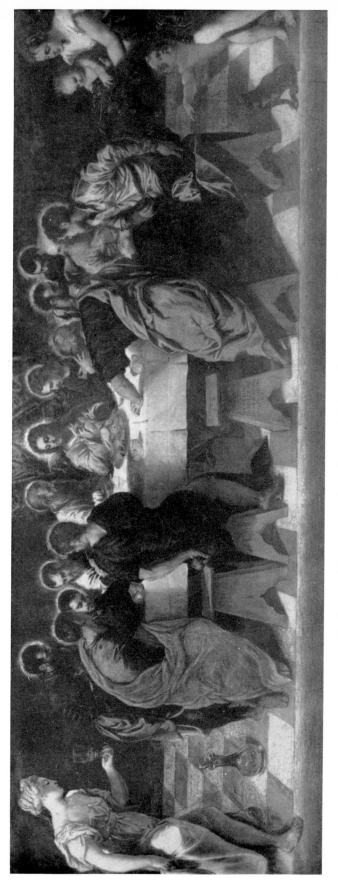

1269. Jacopo Tintoretto: *Last Supper*. S. Marcuola, Venice. *Dated 1547.*

1270. JACOPO TINTORETTO: *Solomon and the Queen of Sheba*. The Bob Jones University Gallery, Greenville (South Carolina).

1271. JACOPO TINTORETTO: *Mark rescuing a Slave*. Accademia, Venice. *Signed. 1548.*

1272. Jacopo Tintoretto: *Christ washing the feet of the Apostles*. Earl of Pembroke and Montgomery, Wilton House (Salisbury).

1273. Jacopo Tintoretto: *Christ washing the feet of the Apostles (from S. Marcuola)*. Prado, Madrid. 1545–50.

1280. Jacopo Tintoretto: *Detail from Plate 1279.*

1281. JACOPO TINTORETTO: *The Creation of the Animals (from the Scuola della Trinità)*. Accademia, Venice. *ca 1550*.

1282. JACOPO TINTORETTO: *The Finding of Moses.* Metropolitan Museum, New York.

1283. Jacopo Tintoretto: *Susanna and the Elders.* Kunsthistorisches Museum, Vienna.

1284. Jacopo Tintoretto: *Joseph and Potiphar's Wife*. Prado, Madrid.

1285. Jacopo Tintoretto: *Venus and Mars with Cupid and the Graces*. Art Institute, Chicago (Illinois).

1286. JACOPO TINTORETTO: *Angel of Annunciation*. Rijksmuseum, Amsterdam.

1287. Jacopo Tintoretto: *Roch visiting the Plague-stricken (detail)*. Choir, S. Rocco, Venice. *?1559*.

1288. Jacopo Tintoretto: *Pietro Pisani*. Homeless.

1289. Jacopo Tintoretto: *Scipione Clusone and his Dwarf*. Homeless. *Signed and dated 1561.*

1290. Jacopo Tintoretto: *Portrait of Youth as David*. Sir Kenneth Clark, Saltwood Castle (Kent).

1291. JACOPO TINTORETTO: *Tarquinius and Lucretia*. Art Institute, Chicago (Illinois).

1292. JACOPO TINTORETTO: *Allegory of Generosity*. Formerly Baron Louis de Rothschild, Vienna.

1293. JACOPO TINTORETTO: *George and the Dragon*. National Gallery, London.

1294. Jacopo Tintoretto: *Sketch for 'The Body of Mark carried away from Alexandria'*
in the Scuola Grande di S. Marco (now Accademia, Venice).
Earl of Crawford, Balcarres (Fife, Scotland). *ca 1562.*

1295. Jacopo Tintoretto: *Sketch for a 'Carrying of Mark's Body to the Ship'.*
Musée Royal des Beaux-Arts, Brussels. *ca 1562.*

1296. Jacopo Tintoretto: *The Law and the Golden Calf (detail)*. Choir, Madonna dell'Orto, Venice.

1297. JACOPO TINTORETTO: *Crucifixion (detail)*. Sala dell'Albergo, Scuola di S. Rocco, Venice.
Signed and dated 1565.

1298. JACOPO TINTORETTO: *Crucifixion* (detail). Sala dell'Albergo, Scuola di S. Rocco, Venice. *Signed and dated 1565.*

1299. Jacopo Tintoretto: *Christ on the road to Calvary*. Sala dell'Albergo, Scuola di S. Rocco, Venice. *1566–67*.

1300. JACOPO TINTORETTO: *Last Supper.* S. Polo, Venice. *1565–70.*

1301. Jacopo Tintoretto: *Baptism*. Museum of Art, Cleveland (Ohio).

1302. JACOPO TINTORETTO: *Allegorical Portrait of Ottavio da Strada*. Rijksmuseum, Amsterdam.
Signed and dated 1567.

1303. JACOPO TINTORETTO: *Christ's Descent into Limbo (detail)*. S. Cassiano, Venice. *1568*.

1304. Jacopo Tintoretto: *A Philosopher*. Libreria Sansoviniana, Venice. *1571–72*.

1305. Jacopo Tintoretto: *A Philosopher* (*detail*). Libreria Sansoviniana, Venice. *1571–72*.

1306. Jacopo Tintoretto and Assistants: *Ceiling: Origin of the Milky Way*. National Gallery, London.

1307. JACOPO TINTORETTO: *Ceiling: Apollo and the Muses*. Bankes Collection,
Kingston Lacy (Wimborne, Dorset).

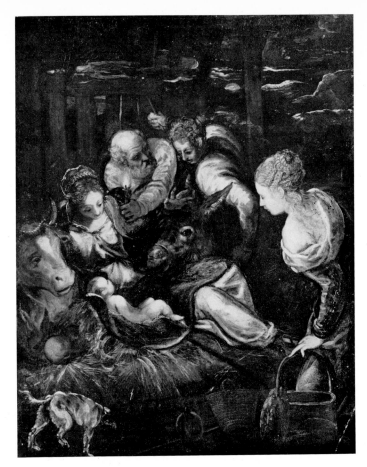

1308. Jacopo Tintoretto: *Sketch for Nativity*. Homeless.

1309. Jacopo Tintoretto: *Samson and Delilah*. Devonshire Collection, Chatsworth.

1310. JACOPO TINTORETTO: *Hercules driving the Faun from the bed of Omphale*. Museum, Budapest.

1311. JACOPO TINTORETTO: *Martyrdom of Lawrence*. Christ Church, Oxford.

1313. Jacopo Tintoretto: *Portrait of a Moor.*
Morgan Library, New York.

1312. Jacopo Tintoretto: *Portrait of a Venetian Senator.*
Homeless.

1315. Jacopo Tintoretto: *Portrait of a Venetian Senator.*
Col. W. Stirling, Keir (Dumblane, Scotland).

1314. Jacopo Tintoretto: *A Procurator of S. Marco.*
Prince Matsukata, Kobi (Japan).

1316. Jacopo Tintoretto: *Sketch for a Conversion of Paul*. S. H. Kress Foundation, New York.

1317. JACOPO TINTORETTO: *Sketch for the 'Capture of Roch at the Battle of Montpellier' in S. Rocco, Venice.* Sir Edward Hulton, London.

1318. JACOPO TINTORETTO: *Sketch for 'Doge Alvise Mocenigo before the Redeemer' in the Palazzo Ducale. Metropolitan Museum, New York. Not later than 1581.*

1319. Jacopo Tintoretto: *Sketch for 'Paradise'.* Louvre, Paris. 1579.

1320. Jacopo Tintoretto: *Detail from Plate 1319.*

1321. Jacopo Tintoretto: *Detail from Plate 1322.*

1322. JACOPO TINTORETTO: *Ascension*. Upper Hall, Scuola di S. Rocco, Venice. *1576–81*.

1323. JACOPO TINTORETTO: *Detail from Plate 1324.*

1324. Jacopo Tintoretto: *Baptism*. Upper Hall, Scuola di S. Rocco, Venice. *1576–81*.

1325. Jacopo Tintoretto: *Nativity*. Upper Hall, Scuola di S. Rocco, Venice. 1576–81.

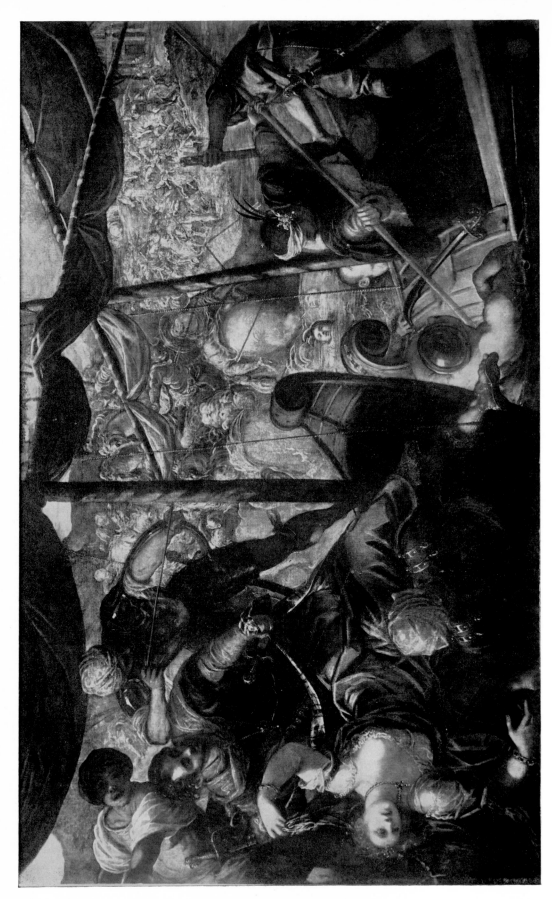

1326. Jacopo Tintoretto: *Battle on land and sea* (*'The Rape of Helen'*). Prado, Madrid.

1327. Jacopo Tintoretto: *Massacre of Innocents*. Ground Floor, Scuola di S. Rocco, Venice. *1583–87*.

1328. Jacopo Tintoretto: *Detail from the Epiphany*. Ground Floor, Scuola di S. Rocco, Venice. 1583–87.

1329. Jacopo Tintoretto: *Flight into Egypt*. Ground Floor, Scuola di S. Rocco, Venice. *1583–87*.

1330. Jacopo Tintoretto: *Mary of Egypt in the Wilderness*.
Ground Floor, Scuola di S. Rocco, Venice. *1583–87*.

1331. Jacopo Tintoretto: *Sketch for Battlescene*. Rhode Island School of Design, Providence (R.I.).

1332. Jacopo Tintoretto: *The Last Supper*. Choir, S. Giorgio Maggiore, Venice. 1594.

1333. JACOPO TINTORETTO: *The Gathering of Manna.* Choir, S. Giorgio Maggiore, Venice. *1592–94.*

View of Venice, 1566.
(Detail from Titian's 'Doge Grimani before Faith' in the Palazzo Ducale.)

TOPOGRAPHICAL INDEX

NOTE

Konopist (Czechoslovakia). All pictures formerly at Konopist Castle are believed to have been transferred to the National Gallery in Prague, but those not mentioned in the Prague catalogue of 1949 have here been listed under Konopist.

Naples, Museo Nazionale. All the pictures are now (since June 1957) at the Pinacoteca, Reggia di Capodimonte.

Paris, Musées Nationaux. Pictures from the Campana Collection, which were distributed among various French provincial museums, have been listed under Paris. It is intended to unite all early Italian pictures from the Campana Collection at Avignon in the near future.

Richmond (Surrey). For the sake of convenient reference, pictures in the Cook Collection have been listed under their old location. The collection has, in fact, been split up and many paintings are on loan to various museums in Britain.

TOPOGRAPHICAL INDEX

Arezzo. PALAZZO PUBBLICO: Sebastiano del Piombo.

Arquà Petrarca (Padua). ORATORIO DELLA SS. TRINITÀ: Veneto-Byzantine Painter.

Arrone (Terni). S. MARIA DELLA QUERCIA: Girolamo da Santacroce.

Aschaffenburg. GEMÄLDEGALERIE: Jacopo Bassano.

Ascoli Piceno. PINACOTECA CIVICA: Alamanno, Carlo Crivelli, Vittorio Crivelli, Titian.

 DUOMO: Carlo Crivelli.

 S. AGOSTINO: Alamanno.

 S. MARIA DELLA CARITÀ: Alamanno.

 SEMINARIO: Alamanno.

Ascott (Bucks.). NATIONAL TRUST: Lotto.

Ashburnham Place (Sussex). LORD ASHBURNHAM (EX): Titian.

Ashby Saint Ledgers (Rugby). VISCOUNT WIMBORNE (EX): Licinio, Pasqualino di Niccolò.

Ashford (Kent). LADY MARCHWOOD: Lotto.

Ashridge Park (Herts.). EARL BROWNLOW (EX): Lotto.

Asiago (Vicenza). CHIESA PARROCCHIALE: Francesco Bassano.

Asola (Mantua). S. ANDREA: Giovanni and Bernardino da Asola.

Asolo (Treviso). MUSEO CIVICO: Dario da Treviso.

 S. MARIA DI BREDA (DUOMO): Andrea da Murano, Jacopo Bassano, Bastiani, Lotto.

Assisi. MRS. F. M. PERKINS: Bonifazio Veronese, Cariani, Rondinelli.

Athens. ROYAL PALACE: Paolo Veronese.

Atlanta (Georgia). ART ASSOCIATION AND HIGH MUSEUM OF ART: Caselli da Parma.

Augsburg. GEMÄLDEGALERIE: Bordone, Sustris.

Autun. MUSÉE: Jacobello del Fiore.

Aviatico (Valle Seriana, Bergamo). S. SALVATORE: Gavazzi.

Avila. CONVENTO DE LAS MADRES: Sebastiano del Piombo.

Bagnarola (Udine). CHIESA PARROCCHIALE: Amalteo.

Bahia (Brazil). SEN. E. C. LOEFF: Lotto.

Balcarres (Fife, Scotland). EARL OF CRAWFORD: Leandro Bassano, Vittore Carpaccio, Savoldo (ex), Tintoretto.

Balduina (Padua). CHIESA PARROCCHIALE: Girolamo di Tommaso da Treviso.

Baltimore (Maryland). WALTERS ART GALLERY: Close to Antonello da Messina, Jaco . . . Bar . . , Basaiti, Leandro Bassano, Giovanni Bellini, Follower of Giovanni Bellini, Bordone, Benedetto Carpaccio, Caselli da Parma, Caterino Veneziano, Catena, Cima, Carlo Crivelli, Vittorio Crivelli, Filippo da Verona, Giambono, Lattanzio da Rimini, Giovanni Martini da Udine, Mazzola, Bartolomeo Montagna, Nicola di Maestro Antonio d'Ancona, Paolo Veronese, Pennacchi, Polidoro, Rondinelli, Francesco da Santacroce, Antonio Solario, Speranza, Tintoretto, Alvise Vivarini, Antonio Vivarini, Bartolomeo Vivarini, Veneto Byzantine Painter.

 MUSEUM OF ART: Tintoretto, Titian.

Barbeano (Udine). S. ANTONIO: Gianfrancesco da Tolmezzo.

Barcelona. MUSEOS DE ARTE, Parque de la Ciudadela: Antonello da Messina, Sebastiano del Piombo, Tintoretto, Bartolomeo Vivarini.

Bari. MUSEO PROVINCIALE: Basaiti, Giovanni Bellini, Bordone, Paolo Veronese, Girolamo da Santacroce, Tintoretto, Antonio Vivarini, Bartolomeo Vivarini.

 S. NICOLA: Bartolomeo Vivarini.

Barlborough Hall (Sheffield). MR. GODFREY LOCKER-LAMPSON (EX): Girolamo da Santacroce.

Barletta (Bari). MUSEO: Giovanni di Francia.

S. ANDREA: Bastiani, Alvise Vivarini.

Barnard Castle (Durham). BOWES MUSEUM: Caprioli, Girolamo di Santacroce.

Baseglia (Udine). S. CROCE: Amalteo.

Basle. MUSEUM: Cariani, Pennacchi, Girolamo da Santacroce.

BACHOFEN FOUNDATION: Diana, Sebastiano del Piombo, Bartolomeo Vivarini.

DR. TOBIAS CHRIST: Nicola di Maestro Antonio d'Ancona.

BARON ROBERT VON HIRSCH: Bonifazio Veronese, Tintoretto.

WENDTLAND COLLECTION (EX): Pasqualino di Niccolò.

Bassanello (Padua). S. MARIA ASSUNTA E S. BELLINO: Mariscalchi.

Bassano del Grappa. MUSEO CIVICO: Francesco Bassano the Elder, Jacopo Bassano, Leandro Bassano, Dario da Treviso, Filippo da Verona, Giovanni Martini da Udine, Pennacchi, Girolamo da Santacroce, Antonio Vivarini, Bartolomeo Vivarini.

DUOMO: Francesco Bassano the Elder, Jacopo Bassano, Leandro Bassano.

S. DONATO: Francesco Bassano the Elder.

CHIESA DELLA BEATA GIOVANNA: Giambono.

S. GIOVANNI BATTISTA: Jacopo Bassano.

S. MARIA DELLE GRAZIE: Jacopo Bassano.

LOGGIA COMUNALE: Jacopo Bassano.

PIAZZA MONTEVECCHIO: Jacopo Bassano.

VIA MATTEOTTI 52: Francesco Bassano the Elder.

Battaglia (Padua). CASTELLO DEL CATAJO: Zelotti.

Bayonne. MUSÉE BONNAT: Cima, Paolo Veronese, Alvise Vivarini.

Beachurst (New York). KARL LOEVENICH COLLECTION: Lotto.

Belgrade. WHITE PALACE: Cariani.

ROYAL PALACE (EX): Lorenzo Veneziano, Palma Vecchio, Paolo Veronese.

Belluno. MUSEO CIVICO: Amalteo, Cesa, Bartolomeo Montagna, Montagnana, Pellegrino da San Daniele, Antonio Solario.

S. MARTINO (DUOMO): Jacopo Bassano, Andrea Schiavone.

S. PIETRO: Andrea Schiavone.

S. STEFANO: Montagnana.

Bennebroek (Haarlem). FRAU VON PANNWITZ (EX): Basaiti.

Bergamo. ACCADEMIA CARRARA: Antonello de Saliba, Bartolomeo Veneto, Basaiti, Jacopo Bassano, Leandro Bassano, Bastiani, Beccaruzzi, Gentile Bellini, Giovanni Bellini, Jacopo Bellini, Belliniano, Bello, Bordone, Buonconsiglio, Cariani, Benedetto Carpaccio, Vittore Carpaccio, Catena, Cima, Carlo Crivelli, Filippo da Verona, Galizzi, Gavazzi, Giorgione Copies, Girolamo da Vicenza, Jacobello di Antonello, Jacopo da Valenza, Licinio, Lotto, Mansueti, Marziale, Bartolomeo Montagna, Palma Vecchio, Paolo Veronese, Polidoro, Pordenone, Previtali, Francesco da Santacroce, Girolamo da Santacroce, Andrea Schiavone, Tintoretto, Francesco Vecellio, Alvise Vivarini, Antonio Vivarini, Bartolomeo Vivarini.

S. ALESSANDRO (DUOMO): Cariani, Previtali.

S. ALESSANDRO IN COLONNA: Leandro Bassano, Gavazzi, Lotto.

S. ALESSANDRO DELLA CROCE: Lotto, Previtali.

S. ANDREA: Previtali.

S. BARTOLOMEO: Lotto.

S. BERNARDINO: Lotto.

CARMINE: Gavazzi.

S. MARIA DEL CONVENTINO: Caselli da Parma, Previtali.

S. MARIA MAGGIORE: Lotto, Previtali.

S. MICHELE DEL POZZO BIANCO: Lotto.

S. SPIRITO: Lotto, Previtali.

AGLIARDI COLLECTION (EX): Basaiti, Galizzi.

SIG. LUIGI FAGIOLI (EX): Lotto.

ARCH. MARIO FRIZZONI: Basaiti, Jacopo Bassano, Bonifazio Veronese, Tintoretto.

FRIZZONI SALIS COLLECTION (EX): Cariani, Bartolomeo Vivarini.

LOCATELLI-MILESI COLLECTION: Lotto.

LOCHIS COLLECTION (EX): Cima.

CONTE MAPELLI (EX): Jacopo Bassano.

CONTE MORONI: Previtali.

PICCINELLI COLLECTION: Girolamo da Treviso.

CONTE RONCALLI: Cariani.

CONTE DINO SECCO SUARDI (EX): Lotto.

CONTE SUARDI: Cariani, Previtali.

SIG. NINO ZUCCHELLI: Cariani.

Berlin. STAATLICHE MUSEEN: Antonello da Messina, Antonello de Saliba, Jacopo de' Barbari, Basaiti, Jacopo Bassano, Bastiani, Gentile Bellini, Giovanni Bellini, Follower of Giovanni Bellini, Bissolo, Bonifazio Veronese, Bordone, Caprioli, Cariani, Benedetto Carpaccio, Vittore Carpaccio, Catena, Cesa, Cima, Carlo Crivelli, Diana, Florigerio, Fogolino, Giorgione, Giovanni and Bernardino da Asola, Girolamo di Tommaso da Treviso, Ingannati, Jacopo da Valenza, Lorenzo Veneziano, Lotto, Mansueti, Marconi, Marziale, Mazzola, Mocetto, Bartolomeo Montagna, Montemezzano, Morto da Feltre, Nicola di Maestro Antonio d'Ancona, Palma Vecchio, Paolo Veronese, Pennacchi, Previtali, Quirizio da Murano, Francesco da Santacroce, Girolamo da Santacroce, Savoldo, Andrea Schiavone, Sebastiano del Piombo, Antonio Solario, Sustris, Tintoretto, Titian, Francesco Vecellio, Alvise Vivarini, Antonio Vivarini, Bartolomeo Vivarini, Venetian fifteenth-century unidentified.

SCHLOSSMUSEUM (EX): Lattanzio da Rimini.

REICHSMINISTERIUM: Bordone.

DR. MAX FRIEDEBERG: Giorgione Copies.

CORAY COLLECTION (EX): Follower of Gentile Bellini.

CONSUL HARRY FULD (EX): Francesco de' Franceschi.

GLOGOWSKI COLLECTION (EX): Mansueti, Tintoretto.

HOLZMANN COLLECTION (EX): Giovanni Bellini.

KAUFMANN COLLECTION (EX): Basaiti, Boldrini, Venetian fifteenth-century unidentified.

SCHWEIZER COLLECTION (EX): Girolamo da Santacroce.

Besançon. MUSÉE DES BEAUX-ARTS: Giovanni Bellini, Cariani, Bartolomeo Montagna, Tintoretto, Titian.

Beziers. MUSÉE DES BEAUX-ARTS: Tintoretto.

Biancade (Venezia). CHIESA PARROCCHIALE: Beccaruzzi.

Billesley Manor (Warwick.). MR. H. G. BOIS (EX): Giovanni Martini da Udine.

Birmingham. BARBER INSTITUTE: Giovanni Bellini, Cima, Paolo Veronese, Tintoretto.

CITY MUSEUM: Bonifazio Veronese, Buonconsiglio, Cima.

Birmingham (Alabama). MUSEUM OF ART: Lattanzio da Rimini, Licinio, Lorenzo Veneziano, Tintoretto.

Blankenburg an der Harz. HERZOG ZU BRAUNSCHWEIG UND LÜNEBURG: Sustris.

Blaschkow (Silesia). MALLMAN COLLECTION (EX): Mancini, Polidoro.

Blenheim Palace (Oxon.). DUKE OF MARLBOROUGH (EX): Bonifazio Veronese.

Bologna. PINACOTECA: Agapiti, Jacopo Bassano, Cima, Giovanni da Bologna, Giovanni and Bernardino da Asola, Lorenzo Veneziano, Tintoretto, Titian, Antonio Vivarini, Bartolomeo Vivarini.

GALLERIA DAVIA-BARGELLINI: Francesco da Santacroce, Antonio Vivarini, Bartolomeo Vivarini.

COLLEZIONI COMUNALI: Campagnola, Tintoretto.

S. COLOMBANO: Agapiti.

S. GIACOMO MAGGIORE: Paolo Veneziano.

S. GIOVANNI IN MONTE: Girolamo di Tommaso da Treviso.

S. PETRONIO: Girolamo di Tommaso da Treviso.

S. SALVATORE: Girolamo di Tommaso da Treviso.

SIG. GIORGIO MORANDI: Jacopo Bassano.

Bonn. PROVINZIALMUSEUM: Leandro Bassano, Bonifazio Veronese, Jacopo da Valenza, Mazzola, Paolo Veronese, Polidoro, Girolamo da Santacroce.

Bordeaux. MUSÉE: Basaiti, Lotto, Paolo Veronese.

Borgo San Sepolcro. PINACOTECA (PALAZZO COMUNALE): Leandro Bassano.

Borso del Grappa (Treviso). CHIESA PARROCCHIALE: Jacopo Bassano.

Boston (Massachusetts). MUSEUM OF FINE ARTS: Basaiti, Jacopo Bassano, Leandro Bassano, Bastiani, Gentile Bellini, Follower of Giovanni Bellini, Bonifazio Veronese, Bordone, Follower of Vittore Carpaccio, Carlo Crivelli, Lotto, Negri, Paolo Veronese, Tintoretto, Titian, Bartolomeo Vivarini.

ISABELLA GARDNER MUSEUM: Bartolomeo Veneto, Gentile Bellini, Giovanni Bellini, Bonifazio Veronese, Bordone, Catena, Cima, Carlo Crivelli, Giambono, Giorgione, Paolo Veronese, Polidoro, Tintoretto, Titian.

QUINCY ADAMS COLLECTION (EX): Cariani.

MR. SUMNER APPLETON (EX): Pordenone.

MRS. EDWARD D. BRANDEGEE: Bonifazio Veronese, Bordone, Licinio.

MRS. JOHN W. ELLIOT (EX): Pasqualino di Niccolò.

MRS. E. HOLMES: Bartolomeo Veneto.

MISS ELIZABETH NORTON: Caprioli, Paolo Veronese.

QUINCY SHAW COLLECTION (EX): Giovanni Bellini, Cima, Mazzola.

WETZEL COLLECTION (EX): Bastiani, Follower of Giovanni Bellini.

Boughton House (Northants.). DUKE OF BUCCLEUCH: Giovanni Bellini.

Bourges. MUSÉE DE BERRY: Tintoretto.

Bovolenta (Padua). CHIESA PARROCCHIALE: Montagnana.

Bowood (Calne, Wilts.). MARQUESS OF LANSDOWNE: Bonifazio Veronese, Giorgione Copies (ex), Oliverio, Sebastiano del Piombo, Titian.

Bracciano (Rome). CASTELLO: Alamanno.

Bratislava. OSMITZ COLLECTION (EX): Lotto.

Braunschweig see **Brunswick.**

Bremen. KUNSTHALLE: Bartolomeo Montagna.

Brescia. PINACOTECA TOSIO MARTINENGO: Bonifazio Veronese, Cariani, Cima, Ingannati, Licinio, Lorenzo Veneziano, Lotto, Palma Vecchio, Paolo da Brescia, Girolamo da Santacroce, Savoldo, Tintoretto.

DUOMO VECCHIO (LA ROTONDA): Licinio.

SEMINARIO DI SANT'ANGELO: Antonio Vivarini.

S. AFRA: Paolo Veronese, Tintoretto.

S. ALESSANDRO: Jacopo Bellini.

SS. NAZZARO E CELSO: Titian.

PALAZZO AVEROLDI (EX): Vittore Carpaccio.

BETTONI COLLECTION (EX): Bastiani.

PALAZZO MARTINENGO SALVADEGO: Lotto.

Breslau. MUSEUM: Buonconsiglio, Marconi, Girolamo da Santacroce.

Bristol. CITY ART GALLERY: Giovanni Bellini, Antonio Solario.

PROF. W. MAC STEWART: Bonifazio Veronese.

Brno see **Brünn.**

Brocklesby Park (Lincs.). EARL OF YARBOROUGH: Tintoretto (ex), Titian.

Brooklyn (New York). BROOKLYN MUSEUM: Bartolomeo Veneto, Giovanni Bellini, Jacopo Bellini, Catena, Cima, Carlo Crivelli, Lotto, Palma Vecchio, Previtali, Tintoretto, Alvise Vivarini.

Brünn. MUSEUM: Antonello de Saliba, Bartolomeo Veneto.

Brunswick. HERZOG ANTON ULRICH MUSEUM: Montemezzano, Palma Vecchio, Paolo Veronese, Tintoretto.

VIEWEG COLLECTION (EX): Pasqualino di Niccolò.

Brussels. MUSÉE ROYAL DES BEAUX-ARTS: Carlo Crivelli, Palma Vecchio, Paolo Veronese, Sustris, Tintoretto.

VAN GELDER COLLECTION (EX): Niccolò de' Barbari, Jacobello del Fiore, Tintoretto.

CHÂTEAU D'ERLE, GOLDSCHMIDT COLLECTION: Jacopo de' Barbari.

SOMZÉE COLLECTION (EX): Polidoro.

Budapest. MUSEUM OF FINE ARTS: Agapiti, Andrea da Murano, Antonello da Messina, Antonio da Carpi, Niccolò de' Barbari, Bartolomeo Veneto, Basaiti, Jacopo Bassano, Beccaruzzi, Gentile Bellini, Follower of Giovanni Bellini, Bello, Bissolo, Bonifazio Veronese, Cariani, Catena, Cima, Carlo Crivelli, Vittorio Crivelli, Francesco de' Franceschi, Giambono, Giorgione, Giorgione Copies, Ingannati, Jacobello del Fiore, Jacopo da Valenza, Licinio, Lotto, Mancini, Marziale, Mazzola, Mocetto, Bartolomeo Montagna, Montagnana, Palma Vecchio, Paolo Veronese, Pietro da Messina, Polidoro, Pordenone, Previtali, Girolamo da Santacroce, Savoldo, Sebastiano del Piombo, Antonio Solario, Speranza, Tintoretto, Titian, Alvise Vivarini, Venetian fifteenth-century unidentified. (Numbers preceded by P refer to pictures from the Pálffy Collection.)

HERR F. GLÜCK (EX): Francesco da Santacroce, Girolamo da Santacroce.

HARTMANN COLLECTION (EX): Tintoretto.

LEDERER COLLECTION (EX): Lotto, Girolamo da Santacroce.

DR. SIMON MELLER (EX): Quirizio da Murano.

Buenos Aires. MR. JORGO BÖHTLINGK: Rondinelli.

Buffalo (New York). ALBRIGHT ART GALLERY: Bastiani.

Buia (Udine). S. LORENZO: Grassi.

Burano see **Venice** (Environs).

Burghley House (Northants.). MARQUESS OF EXETER: Jacopo Bassano, Paolo Veronese.

Burgos. MUSEO: Leandro Bassano.

CATEDRAL: Sebastiano del Piombo.

Bury St. Edmunds see **Ickworth.**

Caen. MUSÉE: Vittore Carpaccio, Cima, Paolo Veronese, Sustris, Tintoretto.

Cambridge. FITZWILLIAM MUSEUM: Bartolomeo Veneto, Basaiti, Jacopo Bassano, Cima, Giovanni and Bernardino da Asola, Palma Vecchio, Paolo Veronese, Polidoro, Francesco da Santacroce, Sebastiano del Piombo, Sustris, Tintoretto, Titian.

Cambridge (Massachusetts). FOGG ART MUSEUM: Antonello de Saliba, Leandro Bassano, Giovanni Bellini, Bordone, Catena, Cima, Carlo Crivelli, Vittorio Crivelli, Girolamo di Tommaso da Treviso, Lattanzio da Rimini, Lotto, Niccolò di Pietro, Palma Vecchio, Paolo Veneziano, Polidoro, Francesco da Santacroce, Tintoretto, Bartolomeo Vivarini.

    MR. J. T. BERGER (EX): Filippo da Verona.

    MR. EDWARD FORBES (EX): Giovanni Bellini.

Campolongo di Conegliano (Treviso). CHIESA PARROCCHIALE: Francesco da Milano.

Camposampiero (Padua). SS. GIOVANNI E ANTONIO: Andrea da Murano, Bonifazio Veronese.

Candide (Belluno). CHIESA PIEVANALE: Francesco Vecellio.

Caneva di Sacile (Udine). CHIESA PARROCCHIALE: Francesco da Milano.

Capesthorne Hall (Cheshire). COL. W. BROMLEY DAVENPORT: Girolamo da Santacroce.

Capetown. SIR JOSEPH ROBINSON (EX): Nicola di Maestro Antonio d'Ancona.

Capodistria. MUSEO CIVICO: Follower of Giovanni Bellini, Benedetto Carpaccio, Vittore Carpaccio, Follower of Vittore Carpaccio, Alvise Vivarini.

    DUOMO: Benedetto Carpaccio, Vittore Carpaccio.

    S. ANNA: Benedetto Carpaccio, Cima, Girolamo da Santacroce.

Carpi. MUSEO CIVICO: Catena.

Carpineta (Cesena). CHIESA PARROCCHIALE: Paolo Veneziano.

Cartigliano (Vicenza). CHIESA PARROCCHIALE: Jacopo Bassano, Bartolomeo Montagna.

Casarsa della Delizia (Udine). PARROCCHIALE NUOVA: Amalteo.

    S. CROCE: Amalteo, Pordenone.

Cassel. GEMÄLDEGALERIE: Leandro Bassano, Lotto, Polidoro, Sustris, Titian.

Cassola (Vicenza). CHIESA PARROCCHIALE: Jacopo Bassano.

Castel Bolognese (Ravenna). S. SEBASTIANO: Girolamo di Tommaso da Treviso.

Castelbuono (Palermo). MATRICE VECCHIA: Antonello de Saliba.

Castel di Mezzo (Pesaro). CHIESA PARROCCHIALE: Jacobello del Fiore.

Castel Folignano (Ascoli). SS. MARIA E CIPRIANO: Alamanno.

Castelfranco Veneto. S. LIBERALE (DUOMO): Jacopo Bassano, Beccaruzzi, Giorgione, Paolo Veronese.

Castellarquato (Piacenza). S. MARIA: Caselli da Parma.

Castello d'Aviano (Udine). S. GREGORIO: Gianfrancesco da Tolmezzo.

Castion (Belluno). CHIESA PARROCCHIALE: Cesa.

Castions di Strada (Udine). S. ANDREA: Amalteo.

Castle Ashby (Northants.). MARQUESS OF NORTHAMPTON: Giovanni Bellini, Girolamo di Tommaso da Treviso, Savoldo. (See also **Compton Wynyates**.)

Castle Howard (Yorks.). MAJOR HOWARD: Leandro Bassano, Giorgione Copies, Licinio (ex).

Castroreale. CHIESA DEL CIMITERO: Antonello de Saliba.

Catania. MUSEO CIVICO DI CASTELLO URSINO: Antonello de Saliba.

Catanzaro. MUSEO PROVINCIALE: Antonello de Saliba.

Cavaso del Tomba (Treviso). CHIESA ARCIPRETALE: Jacopo Bassano.

    CHIESA PARROCCHIALE: Francesco da Milano.

Cefalù (Palermo). MUSEO DELLA FONDAZIONE MANDRALISCA: Antonello da Messina.

Celana (Caprino Bergamasco). S. MARIA ASSUNTA: Lotto.

Cerreto di Venarotta (Ascoli). S. SALVATORE: Alamanno.

Châalis (Ermenonville). MUSÉE JACQUEMART-ANDRÉ: Agostini, Mansueti.

Chailey (Sussex). MR. H. ASA THOMAS (EX): Jacopo da Valenza.

Chantilly. MUSÉE CONDÉ: Catena, Mancini, Palma Vecchio.

Charlbury (Oxon.). MRS. BULLER: Cariani.

Chatsworth (Derbyshire). DEVONSHIRE COLLECTION: Bordone, Cariani, Paolo Veronese, Andrea Schiavone, Sustris, Tintoretto.

Chenonceaux (Tours). CHÂTEAU, MME GEORGES MENIER: Tintoretto.

Cherso (Istria). COLLEGIATA: Alvise Vivarini.

Chicago (Illinois). ART INSTITUTE: Jacopo Bassano, Follower of Gentile Bellini, Giovanni Bellini, Follower of Giovanni Bellini, Carlo Crivelli, Palma Vecchio, Paolo Veneziano, Paolo Veronese, Girolamo da Santacroce, Sustris, Tintoretto, Titian.

 MR. EDWARDS: Tintoretto.

 J. W. ELLSWORTH COLLECTION (EX): Lotto.

 LAKE FOREST, JOHN R. THOMPSON COLLECTION (EX). Giovanni Bellini, Bissolo.

Chioggia (Venice). MUNICIPIO: Jacobello del Fiore.

 S. DOMENICO: Leandro Bassano, Vittore Carpaccio.

 ORATORIO DI SAN MARTINO: Paolo Veneziano.

Chiuduno (Bergamo). DOTT. ERNESTO SUARDO: Jacopo Bassano.

Cincinnati (Ohio): MUSEUM OF ART: Titian.

Cingoli (Macerata). S. ESUPERANZIO: Agapiti, Antonio da Faenza.

 S. DOMENICO: Lotto.

Cintra (Portugal). OLD PALACE: Bordone.

Città di Castello. PINACOTECA CIVICA: Francesco de' Franceschi, Antonio Vivarini.

Cittadella (Padua). CHIESA PARROCCHIALE: Jacopo Bassano, Montagnana.

Civezzano (Trento). CHIESA PARROCCHIALE: Jacopo Bassano.

Cividale del Friuli (Udine). ASSUNTA (DUOMO): Amalteo, Pordenone.

 MUSEO ARCHEOLOGICO: Pellegrino da San Daniele.

 S. MARIA DEI BATTUTI: Pellegrino da San Daniele.

Cleveland (Ohio). MUSEUM OF ART: Bartolomeo Veneto, Jacopo Bassano, Leandro Bassano, Cima, Carlo Crivelli, Filippo da Verona, Lotto, Paolo Veronese, Savoldo, Tintoretto, Titian.

 MRS. WILLIAM G. MATHER: Mancini.

Clouds (Salisbury, Wilts.). CAPTAIN RICHARD WYNDHAM (EX): Licinio.

Collalto (Colle di S. Salvatore, Susegana). CAPPELLA DEL CASTELLO (EX): Mansueti, Pordenone.

Cologna Veneta (Verona). S. MARIA (DUOMO): Bartolomeo Montagna.

Cologne. WALLRAF-RICHARTZ MUSEUM: Bordone, Jacobello del Fiore (ex), Sustris.

Cologny (Geneva). BODMER COLLECTION: Buonconsiglio.

Columbia (South Carolina). MUSEUM OF ART: Tintoretto, Venetian fifteenth-century unidentified.

Columbus (Ohio). GALLERY OF FINE ARTS, F. W. SCHUMACHER COLLECTION: Jacopo da Valenza, Bartolomeo Montagna, Montagnana, Previtali, Girolamo da Santacroce, Sebastiano del Piombo.

 MR. F. W. SCHUMACHER: Tintoretto, Venetian sixteenth-century unidentified.

Comisa see **Komiza.**

Compton Wynyates (Warwicks.). MARQUESS OF NORTHAMPTON: Caselli da Parma, Giorgionesque Paintings. (See also **Castle Ashby.**)

Conegliano (Treviso). CASTELVECCHIO: Pordenone.

 S. MARIA DEI BATTUTI E S. LEONARDO (DUOMO): Cima.

SALA DEI BATTUTI: Beccaruzzi, Francesco da Milano, Previtali.

S. MARIA DELLE GRAZIE: Beccaruzzi.

S. MARTINO: Francesco da Milano.

VIA XX SETTEMBRE, NO. 237: Girolamo da Treviso.

BORGO DELLA MADONNA, CASA CARPENÈ: Dario da Treviso.

Constantinople. SERAI LIBRARY: Gentile Bellini.

UNIVERSITY LIBRARY: Follower of Gentile Bellini.

Copenhagen. STATE MUSEUM OF ART: Jacopo Bassano, Cima, Giorgione Copies, Ingannati, Lotto, Antonio Solario, Tintoretto, Titian.

MARGARET PETERSEN COLLECTION: Sebastiano del Piombo.

(ENVIRONS). NAESTVED, GAUNÖE COLLECTION: Tintoretto.

Corbolone (Treviso). S. MARCO: Pordenone.

Cordova. MUSEO PROVINCIAL: Leandro Bassano.

Cornbury Park (Charlbury, Oxon.). MR. OLIVER VERNON WATNEY: Jacopo Bassano, Giovanni Bellini, Bordone, Lotto, Nicola di Maestro Antonio d'Ancona, Sebastiano del Piombo, Tintoretto (ex).

Cornedo (Vicenza). CHIESA PARROCCHIALE: Buonconsiglio.

Corridonia (Macerata). S. AGOSTINO: Carlo Crivelli.

SS. PIETRO E. PAOLO: Antonio Vivarini, Bartolomeo Vivarini.

Corsham Court (Wilts.). LORD METHUEN: Bonifazio Veronese.

Cortemaggiore (Piacenza). CHIESA DEI FRANCESCANI: Mazzola, Pordenone.

Costa di Mezzate (Bergamo). CASTELLO, CONTESSA CAMOZZI: Lotto.

Costozza (Vicenza). VILLA DEI CARLI: Zelotti.

Cracow. CZARTORYSKI MUSEUM: Alamanno, Follower of Giovanni Bellini, Bonifazio Veronese, Catena, Lorenzo Veneziano, Mazzola, Palma Vecchio.

PRINCE CASIMIR LUBOMIRSKI (EX): Leandro Bassano, Montemezzano.

COUNT SIGISMUND PUSLOWSKI (EX): Lotto.

Credaro (Bergamo). S. GIORGIO: Lotto.

Crema (Cremona). S. MARIA DELLA CROCE: Diana.

Cremona. MUSEO CIVICO: Niccolò de' Barbari, Bissolo, Diana, Giovanni and Bernardino da Asola, Girolamo di Tommaso da Treviso, Mansueti, Mazzola, Francesco da Santacroce.

DUOMO: Pordenone.

Crichel (Wimborne, Dorset). THE HON. MRS. MARTEN: Andrea Schiavone.

Crosara see **San Luca di Crosara.**

Culver (Indiana). MILITARY ACADEMY: Bartolomeo Veneto.

Cupra Marittima (Ascoli Piceno). CHIESA PARROCCHIALE: Alamanno.

Curzola (Dalmatia) see **Korčula.**

Cusio (Bergamo). S. MARGHERITA: Previtali.

Dallas (Texas). MUSEUM OF FINE ARTS: Bordone, Titian.

Darmstadt. LANDESMUSEUM: Jacopo da Valenza, Paolo Veronese.

Denver (Colorado). ART MUSEUM: Antonello da Messina, Vittore Carpaccio, Carlo Crivelli, Giovanni da Bologna, Alvise Vivarini.

Detroit (Michigan). INSTITUTE OF ARTS: Agostini, Antonello de Saliba, Jacopo Bassano, Leandro Bassano, Giovanni Bellini, Caselli da Parma, Cima, Carlo Crivelli, Francesco de' Franceschi, Giambono, Lorenzo Veneziano, Niccolò di Pietro, Palma Vecchio, Paolo Veronese, Previtali, Sebastiano del Piombo, Sustris, Tintoretto, Titian.

MR. L. P. FISHER: Bartolomeo Veneto.

MRS. EDSEL FORD: Bartolomeo Veneto, Tintoretto, Titian.

MRS. LILIAN HENKEL HAAS: Paolo Veronese.

Dijon. MUSÉE DES BEAUX-ARTS: Bartolomeo Veneto, Jacopo Bassano, Leandro Bassano, Follower of Giovanni Bellini, Boldrini, Giovanni and Bernardino da Asola, Lotto, Palma Vecchio, Paolo Veronese, Tintoretto, Titian.

Domegge (Belluno). S. ROCCO: Francesco Vecellio.

Dont (Belluno). CASA BRUSTOLON (EX): Antonio Rosso da Cadore.

Dortmund. DR. WALTER SCHLUTER (EX): Previtali.

Dossena (Bergamo). CHIESA PARROCCHIALE: Paolo Veronese, Francesco da Santacroce.

Douai. MUSÉE: Bartolomeo Veneto, Paolo Veronese.

Drayton House (Northants.). STOPFORD SACKVILLE COLLECTION (EX): Catena.

Dresden. GEMÄLDEGALERIE: Antonello da Messina, Jacopo de' Barbari, Bartolomeo Veneto, Jacopo Bassano, Leandro Bassano, Gentile Bellini, Giovanni Bellini, Bonifazio Veronese, Bordone, Catena, Cima, Giorgione, Giorgione Copies, Girolamo di Tommaso da Treviso, Ingannati, Licinio, Lotto, Mancini, Mariscalchi, Marziale, Montemezzano, Palma Vecchio, Paolo Veronese, Polidoro, Pordenone, Previtali, Girolamo da Santacroce, Andrea Schiavone, Tintoretto, Titian, Francesco Vecellio, Zelotti.

Dublin. NATIONAL GALLERY OF IRELAND: Jacopo Bassano, Bastiani, Giovanni Bellini, Bonifazio Veronese, Bordone, Catena, Mariscalchi, Oliverio, Paolo Veronese, Girolamo da Santacroce, Savoldo, Sebastiano del Piombo, Sustris, Tintoretto, Titian.

MR. J. A. MURNAGHAN: Bonifazio Veronese, Cariani, Girolamo di Tommaso da Treviso, Girolamo da Santacroce, Savoldo.

Dubrovnik. MUSEO: Paris Bordone.

PALAZZO DEI RETTORI: Bordone.

CATTEDRALE: Catena, Savoldo, Titian.

S. DOMENICO: Titian.

Dulwich. COLLEGE GALLERY: Paolo Veronese.

Duncombe Park (Yorks.). EARL OF FEVERSHAM: Girolamo da Santacroce.

Düsseldorf. KUNSTAKADEMIE: Giovanni Bellini, Bissolo, Cima, Montemezzano.

Eastnor Castle (Hereford). HON. MRS. HERVEY BATHURST: Giovanni Bellini, Lotto.

LORD SOMERS (EX): Tintoretto.

Ecton Hall (Northants.). SOTHEBY COLLECTION (EX): Tintoretto.

Edenbridge (Kent). MR. ARCHIBALD WERNER: Jacopo Bassano, Palma Vecchio.

Edinburgh. NATIONAL GALLERY OF SCOTLAND: Jacopo Bassano, Bordone, Cima, Giorgionesque Paintings, Ingannati, Paolo Veronese, Polidoro, Tintoretto, Francesco Vecellio.

— ELLESMERE LOAN: Lotto, Tintoretto, Titian. (See also **Mertoun House.**)

UNIVERSITY: Paolo Veronese.

Eltville (Rhein). GRÄFIN FRANCHEN-SIERSTORPFF (EX): Tintoretto.

Enego (Vicenza). CHIESA ARCIPRETALE: Jacopo Bassano.

Englewood (New Jersey). MRS. DAN FELLOWS PLATT: Vittorio Crivelli, Mazzola, Previtali.

PLATT COLLECTION (EX): Florigerio, Jacobello del Fiore, Lattanzio da Rimini, Giovanni Martini da Udine.

Enschede (Holland). RIJKSMUSEUM TWENTHE: Bartolomeo Vivarini.

Escurial. PALACIO REAL: Titian.

CHAPTER HALL: Paolo Veronese, Tintoretto, Titian.

UPPER CLOISTER: Titian.

IGLESIA VIEJA: Titian.

Este. CHIESA DEGLI ZOCCOLI: Cima.

Esztergom (Hungary). GALLERY OF THE PRINCE PRIMATE: Vittorio Crivelli, Lorenzo Veneziano, Polidoro, Antonio Vivarini.

Eynsham (Oxon.). MRS. PARKINSON (EX): Paolo Veronese.

Fabriano. MUSEO CIVICO: Filippo da Verona.

Faenza. PINACOTECA: Andrea da Murano.

CHIESA DELLA COMMENDA: Girolamo di Tommaso da Treviso.

Falerone (Ascoli). S. FORTUNATO: Vittorio Crivelli.

Fano. MUSEO CIVICO MALATESTIANO: Giambono.

Fanzolo (Treviso). VILLA EMO: Zelotti.

Farnham (Ireland). LORD FARNHAM (EX): Tintoretto.

Farra (Belluno). S. MARTINO: Mariscalchi.

Feltre (Belluno). PINACOTECA: Gentile Bellini, Giovanni Bellini, Cima, Mariscalchi, Morto da Feltre, Pellegrino da San Daniele.

S. PIETRO (DUOMO): Mariscalchi.

S. LORENZO (BATTISTERO): Leandro Bassano.

S. GIACOMO MAGGIORE: Amalteo.

S. MARIA DEGLI ANGELI: Jacopo Bassano, Mariscalchi.

OGNISSANTI: Morto da Feltre.

CASA TAURO: Morto da Feltre.

Fermo (Ascoli). PINACOTECA CIVICA: Giovanni di Francia, Jacobello del Fiore, Veneto-Byzantine Painters unidentified.

S. LUCIA: Vittorio Crivelli.

S. MARIA DEL CARMINE: Antonio Solario.

S. MARIA IN CAPODARCO: Vittorio Crivelli.

S. MICHELE ARCANGELO: Jacobello di Bonomo.

Ferrara. PINACOTECA COMUNALE: Beccaruzzi, Vittore Carpaccio.

MASSARI ZAVAGLIA COLLECTION (EX): Carrari da Forlì.

VENDEGHINI COLLECTION: Jacopo Bellini.

Filacciano (Rome). CASTELLO: Domenico di Candido da Tolmezzo.

Firle Place (Sussex). VISCOUNTESS GAGE: Tintoretto.

Florence. GALLERIA DEGLI UFFIZI: Bartolomeo Veneto, Jacopo Bassano, Leandro Bassano, Beccaruzzi, Giovanni Bellini, Jacopo Bellini, Bonifazio Veronese, Bordone, Vittore Carpaccio, Cima, Duia, Florigerio, Giorgione, Licinio, Lotto, Mansueti, Oliverio, Palma Vecchio, Paolo Veronese, Polidoro, Pordenone, Savoldo, Sebastiano del Piombo, Tintoretto, Titian, Bartolomeo Vivarini.

GALLERIA PALATINA DI PALAZZO PITTI: Leandro Bassano, Bonifazio Veronese, Bordone, Giorgione, Licinio, Paolo Veronese, Polidoro, Pordenone, Andrea Schiavone, Sebastiano del Piombo, Sustris, Tintoretto, Titian.

GALLERIA CORSINI: Giovanni Bellini.

GALLERIA DI CASA BUONARROTI: Titian.

MUSEO HORNE: Cima.

MUSEO STIBBERT: Carlo Crivelli.

MUSEO BARDINI: Giambono.

PALAZZO STROZZI, CENTRO NAZIONALE DI STUDI SUL RINASCIMENTO: Andrea Schiavone.

PALAZZO VECCHIO: Paolo Veronese, Polidoro, Tintoretto.

BARTOLOMMEI COLLECTION: Lotto.

BERENSON COLLECTION: Alamanno, Giovanni Bellini, Jacopo Bellini, Bello, Bonifazio Veronese, Bordone, Cima, Giambono, Gianfrancesco da Tolmezzo, Jacobello del Fiore, Lotto, Sebastiano del Piombo.

CONTINI BONACOSSI COLLECTION: Bartolomeo Veneto, Jacopo Bassano, Giovanni Bellini, Vittore Carpaccio, Catena, Cima, Carlo Crivelli, Lorenzo Veneziano, Lotto, Mazzola, Palma Vecchio, Paolo Veronese, Savoldo, Sebastiano del Piombo, Tintoretto, Titian, Bartolomeo Vivarini.

CONTE CARLO GAMBA: Mancini.

GUALINO COLLECTION: Lotto.

BARON VON HADELN (EX): Lotto, Tintoretto.

LOESER COLLECTION (EX): Giovanni Bellini, Giorgione Copies, Paolo Veneziano, Girolamo da Santacroce, Andrea Schiavone.

PROF. R. LONGHI: Cariani, Diana, Jacobello del Fiore, Sustris.

MARCHESE NICCOLINI DI CAMUGLIANO: Giovanni Bellini.

PANCIATICHI COLLECTION (EX): Lotto.

SERRISTORI COLLECTION: Antonello de Saliba, Vittore Carpaccio, Mazzola, Quirizio da Murano.

SEVERINO SPINELLI (EX): Agostini, Leandro Bassano, Giovanni and Bernardino da Asola, Montemezzano, Andrea Schiavone.

GALLERIA FERRONI (CENACOLO DI FOLIGNO): Lotto.

(ENVIRONS). PRATOLINO, PRINCE PAUL OF YUGOSLAVIA: Andrea Schiavone, Titian.

Follina (Treviso). ABBAZIA: Francesco da Milano.

Forlì. PINACOTECA: Carrari da Forlì, Filippo da Verona, Rondinelli.

DUOMO: Rondinelli.

S. MERCURIALE: Rondinelli.

Forni di Sopra (Udine). S. FLORIANO A CELLA: Bellunello, Gianfrancesco da Tolmezzo.

S. MARIA ASSUNTA: Domenico di Candido da Tolmezzo.

Forni di Sotto (Udine). S. LORENZO: Gianfrancesco da Tolmezzo.

Forza d'Agrò (Messina). CHIESA DELLA TRIADE: Antonello de Saliba.

Foza (Vicenza). CHIESA PARROCCHIALE: Francesco Bassano the Elder.

Frankfurt am Main. STÄDELSCHES INSTITUT: Antonello de Saliba, Bartolomeo Veneto, Giovanni Bellini, Vittore Carpaccio, Catena, Cima, Carlo Crivelli, Giorgionesque Furniture Painter, Palma Vecchio, Tintoretto, Titian.

BARON ROBERT VON HIRSCH see **Basle.**

MR. EDGAR SPEYER (EX): Girolamo da Santacroce.

Gaggio (Venice). CHIESA PARROCCHIALE: Bissolo.

Gallodoro (Messina). CHIESA PARROCCHIALE: Antonello de Saliba.

Garrowby Hall (Yorks.). EARL OF HALIFAX: Titian.

Gatchina see **Leningrad.**

Gazzada (Varese). CAGNOLA COLLECTION: Antonello de Saliba, Jacopo Bellini, Licinio, Antonio Vivarini, Bartolomeo Vivarini.

Gemona (Udine). PALAZZO DEL COMUNE: Gianfrancesco da Tolmezzo.

DUOMO: Grassi.

S. GIOVANNI: Amalteo.

S. MARIA DELLE GRAZIE: Cima, Pellegrino da San Daniele.

S. ROCCO: Pordenone.

Geneva. MUSÉE D'ART ET D'HISTOIRE: Paolo Veronese.

Genoa. PALAZZO BIANCO: Leandro Bassano, Palma Vecchio, Paolo Veronese.

PALAZZO REALE: Bordone, Tintoretto.

PALAZZO ROSSO: Bordone, Licinio, Paolo Veronese, Titian.

SS. ANNUNZIATA: Bissolo.

A. BASEVI COLLECTION: Lotto.

G. CARPANETO DEI MARCHESI SPINOLA (EX): Girolamo da Santacroce.

GALLERIA SPINOLA: Antonello da Messina.

AMBROGIO DORIA COLLECTION: Bartolomeo Veneto, Bordone, Paolo Veronese.

DORIA-BALBI COLLECTION: Bordone, Titian.

DURAZZO ADORNO COLLECTION: Giovanni and Bernardino da Asola.

PRINCIPESSA PALLAVICINI: Follower of Vittore Carpaccio.

SIG. M. C. VIEZZOLI: Cariani, Savoldo.

Ghent. MUSÉE: Tintoretto.

Giovinazzo (Bari). CATTEDRALE: Jacobello del Fiore.

S. DOMENICO: Lotto.

Glasgow. CORPORATION ART GALLERIES: Bartolomeo Veneto, Giovanni Bellini, Bordone, Catena, Giorgione, Bartolomeo Montagna, Oliverio, Palma Vecchio, Polidoro, Tintoretto.

COATES COLLECTION (EX): Basaiti.

Glen Falls (New York). MRS. LOUIS HYDE: Tintoretto.

Gleris (Udine). CHIESA PARROCCHIALE: Amalteo.

Gosford House (Haddington, East Lothian, Scotland). EARL OF WEMYSS: Bordone, Girolamo da Santacroce, Savoldo, Andrea Schiavone.

Gotha. LANDESMUSEUM: Marconi.

Gothenburg. MUSEUM: Jacopo Bassano, Paris Bordone, Tintoretto.

Göttingen. UNIVERSITÄT: Cesa, Cima, Mansueti.

Gradara (Pesaro). RACCOLTA CIVICA: Venetian fifteenth-century unidentified.

Graz. JOHANNEUM: Leandro Bassano, Licinio, Andrea Schiavone.

PALAIS ATTEMS: Leandro Bassano, Bordone.

Greenville (South Carolina). THE BOB JONES UNIVERSITY GALLERY: Bonifazio Veronese, Paolo Veronese, Tintoretto.

Grenoble. MUSÉE DES BEAUX-ARTS: Jacopo Bassano, Licinio, Palma Vecchio, Paolo Veronese, Tintoretto.

Grittleton (Chippenham, Wilts.). SIR AUDLEY NEELD (EX): Cariani.

Grottaferrata (Rome). CONTESSA SENNI: Niccolò di Pietro.

Gualdo Tadino (Perugia). PINACOTECA: Girolamo da Santacroce.

Gubbio. PINACOTECA COMUNALE: Alamanno, Buscatti, Vittorio Crivelli.

Haddington see **Gosford House.**

The Hague. MAURITSHUIS: Jacopo de'Barbari.

BACHSTITZ COLLECTION (EX): Tintoretto.

Hamble (Hampshire). DR. EMMONS: Paolo Veronese.

Hamburg. KUNSTHALLE: Buonconsiglio, Lotto.

WEDELLS COLLECTION (EX): Giovanni Bellini, Bordone.

Hampton Court. ROYAL COLLECTIONS: Jacopo Bassano, Leandro Bassano, Giovanni Bellini, Bonifazio Veronese, Bordone, Cariani, Cima, Giorgione, Girolamo di Tommaso da Treviso, Licinio, Lotto, Palma Vecchio, Paolo Veronese, Pordenone, Savoldo, Andrea Schiavone, Sustris, Tintoretto, Titian, Francesco Vecellio, Alvise Vivarini.

Hanover. KESTNER MUSEUM: Rondinelli, Tintoretto.

DUKE OF CUMBERLAND (EX): Mancini.

Harewood House (Yorks.). EARL OF HAREWOOD: Giovanni Bellini, Bordone, Cima, Diana, Lotto, Oliverio, Paolo Veronese, Sebastiano del Piombo, Tintoretto, Titian, Antonio Vivarini.

Hartford (Conn.). WADSWORTH ATHENEUM: Leandro Bassano, Follower of Giovanni Bellini, Paolo Veneziano, Previtali, Tintoretto.

Haughton Hall (Cheshire). BROCKLEBANK COLLECTION (EX): Buonconsiglio.

Havana (Cuba). MUSEUM: Jacopo Bassano.

s'Heerenberg (Arnhem). VAN HEEK COLLECTION (EX): Vittorio Crivelli.

Heidelberg. VON FOERSTER COLLECTION: Belliniano.

Hermannstadt see **Sibiu.**

Highnam Court (Glos.). GAMBIER-PARRY COLLECTION: Follower of Gentile Bellini, Bartolomeo Montagna, Nicola di Maestro Antonio d'Ancona, Polidoro, Girolamo da Santacroce.

Hopetoun House (Edinburgh). MARQUESS OF LINLITHGOW: Venetian sixteenth-century unidentified.

Horsmonden (Kent). AUSTEN COLLECTION (EX): Bissolo, Filippo da Verona, Licinio.

Houston (Texas). MUSEUM OF FINE ARTS: Bartolomeo Veneto, Giovanni Bellini, Catena, Lotto, Paolo Veronese, Tintoretto, Francesco Vecellio, Antonio Vivarini.

Hull (Yorks.). ART GALLERY: Francesco da Santacroce.

Hurn Court (Christchurch, Hants.). EARL OF MALMESBURY (EX): Giorgione Copies.

Ickworth (Suffolk). NATIONAL TRUST: Titian.

Illeggio (Udine). S. FLORIANO: Domenico di Candido da Tolmezzo.

Imola (Environs). RIVIERA DI CASTELFIUMANESE, CHIESA PARROCCHIALE: Agapiti.

Indianapolis (Indiana). JOHN HERRON ART INSTITUTE: Rondinelli, Titian.

DR. G. H. A. CLOWES: Follower of Giovanni Bellini, Tintoretto, Titian.

MRS. BOOTH TARKINGTON: Alvise Vivarini.

Innsbruck. FERDINANDEUM: Rondinelli.

Invillino (Udine). ANTICA PIEVE: Domenico di Candido da Tolmezzo.

Isola Bella (Lago Maggiore). PALAZZO BORROMEO: Bordone, Ingannati.

Isola d'Istria. DUOMO: Girolamo da Santacroce.

Jesi. PINACOTECA CIVICA: Agapiti, Lotto, Nicola di Maestro Antonio d'Ancona.

Kansas City (Missouri). NELSON GALLERY AND ATKINS MUSEUM: Giovanni Bellini, Vittore Carpaccio, Carlo Crivelli, Vittorio Crivelli, Giovanni and Bernardino da Asola, Paolo Veronese, Previtali, Girolamo da Santacroce, Titian.

Karlsruhe. GEMÄLDEGALERIE: Vittore Carpaccio, Girolamo da Santacroce.

Keir (Dunblane, Scotland). COL. W. STIRLING: Beccaruzzi, Bordone, Tintoretto.

Kenosha (Wisconsin). HEIRS OF MR. NATHAN ALLEN: Titian.

Kiel. MARTIUS COLLECTION: Sebastiano del Piombo.

Kiev. MUSEUM: Giovanni Bellini.

Kingston Lacy (Wimborne, Dorset). MR. BANKES: Giorgione, Tintoretto, Titian.

Kinmel (Abergele, North Wales). H. R. HUGHES COLLECTION (EX): Lotto.

Klosterneuburg. MONASTERY MUSEUM: Bastiani, Girolamo da Santacroce.

Kobi (Japan). PRINCE MATSUKATA: Tintoretto.

Komiza (Island of Vis, Dalmatia). DUOMO PARROCCHIALE: Vittorio Crivelli.

Konopist (Czechoslovakia). CASTLE: Francesco de' Franceschi, Montagnana, Quirizio da Murano, Bartolomeo Vivarini. See also **Prague.**

Korčula (Dalmatia). DUOMO: Leandro Bassano.
CHIESA DELLA CONCEZIONE: Jacobello del Fiore, Mancini.
OGNISSANTI: Jacobello del Fiore.

Kremsier (Czechoslovakia). ARCHIEPISCOPAL GALLERY: Jacopo Bassano, Titian.

Lagosta (Dalmatia). DUOMO: Bissolo, Girolamo da Santacroce.

Lambton Castle (Durham). EARL OF DURHAM (EX): Sebastiano del Piombo.

Lamon (Belluno). CHIESA PARROCCHIALE: Mariscalchi.

Lanciano (Chieti). S. MARIA MAGGIORE: Girolamo da Santacroce.
S. NICOLA: Polidoro.

Lancut. POTOCKI COLLECTION (EX): Giovanni Bellini.

Langres. MUSÉE SAINT-DIDIER: Basaiti.

Langton (Berwickshire, Scotland). MRS. BAILLIE-HAMILTON (EX): Sebastiano del Piombo.

Lapedona (Ascoli). S. GIACOMO: Alamanno.

Latisana (Udine). CHIESA PARROCCHIALE: Paolo Veronese.

La Valetta (Malta). MUSEO: Beccaruzzi, Mansueti.
MR. J. A. CANCHI: Andrea Schiavone.

Lawrence (Kansas). UNIVERSITY MUSEUM OF ART: Tintoretto.

Lecce. MUSEO PROVINCIALE: Girolamo da Santacroce, Antonio Vivarini, Bartolomeo Vivarini, Veneto-Byzantine Painter.

Leipzig. MUSEUM: Bissolo, Tintoretto.
HARCK COLLECTION: Cima.
PROF. THIEME (EX): Pennacchi.

Lendinara (Rovigo). SANTUARIO DELLA MADONNA DEL PILASTRELLO: Montemezzano, Paolo Veronese.
S. SOFIA (DUOMO): Bissolo, Mancini.

Leningrad. HERMITAGE: Bartolomeo Veneto, Jacopo Bassano, Leandro Bassano, Bello, Bonifazio Veronese, Bordone, Caprioli, Cariani, Follower of Vittore Carpaccio, Catena, Cima, Giorgione, Giorgione Copies, Giorgionesque Paintings, Licinio, Lotto, Marconi, Mariscalchi, Palma Vecchio, Paolo Veronese, Pasqualino di Niccolò, Francesco da Santacroce, Girolamo da Santacroce, Sebastiano del Piombo, Sustris, Tintoretto, Titian, Francesco Vecellio, Alvise Vivarini, Zelotti.
LEUCHTENBERG COLLECTION (EX): Bordone, Catena.

Lentiai (Belluno). CHIESA ARCIPRETALE: Giovanni da Mel.

Le Puy. MUSÉE CROZATIER: Jacobello del Fiore.

Lestans (Udine). CHIESA PARROCCHIALE: Amalteo.

Lewes (Sussex). MR. E. P. WARREN (EX): Bello.

Lichtenwalde (Saxony). VITZTHUM VON ECKSTADT COLLECTION: Francesco da Milano.

Lille. MUSÉE: Leandro Bassano, Bonifazio Veronese, Ingannati, Jacobello del Fiore, Paolo Veronese, Polidoro, Sustris, Tintoretto, Zelotti.

Linköping (Sweden). MUSEUM: Ingannati.

Linz. LANDESMUSEUM: Ingannati.

Lisbon. GULBENKIAN FOUNDATION: Vittore Carpaccio, Cima.

Little Rock (Arkansas). FINE ARTS CLUB: Leandro Bassano.

Liverpool. WALKER ART GALLERY: Basaiti, Jacopo Bassano, Giovanni Bellini, Bonifazio Veronese, Catena, Fogolino, Ingannati, Paolo Veronese, Girolamo da Santacroce.

Lockinge House (Wantage, Berks.). MR. CHRISTOPHER LOYD: Cima, Licinio, Girolamo da Santacroce.

London. NATIONAL GALLERY: Andrea da Murano, Antonello da Messina, Close to Antonello da Messina, Jacopo de' Barbari, Bartolomeo Veneto, Basaiti, Jacopo Bassano, Leandro Bassano, Bastiani, Gentile Bellini, Giovanni Bellini, Bissolo, Bonifazio Veronese, Bordone, Buonconsiglio, Busati, Cariani, Vittore Carpaccio, Catena, Cima, Carlo Crivelli, Diana, Giambono, Giorgione, Giorgione Copies, Giorgionesque Paintings, Giorgionesque Furniture Painters, Giovanni and Bernardino da Asola, Girolamo di Tommaso da Treviso, Girolamo da Vicenza, Ingannati, Licinio, Lorenzo Veneziano, Lotto, Mansueti, Giovanni Martini da Udine, Marziale, Mazzola, Mocetto, Bartolomeo Montagna, Palma Vecchio, Paolo Veronese, Pordenone, Previtali, Girolamo da Santacroce, Savoldo, Andrea Schiavone, Sebastiano del Piombo, Antonio Solario, Sustris, Tacconi, Tintoretto, Titian, Alvise Vivarini, Antonio Vivarini, Bartolomeo Vivarini, Zelotti.

BRITISH MUSEUM: Jacopo Bellini.

UNIVERSITY, LEE OF FAREHAM COLLECTION: Bastiani, Giovanni Bellini, Cima, Francesco de' Franceschi, Giorgionesque Paintings, Giovanni and Bernardino da Asola, Palma Vecchio, Paolo Veneziano, Paolo Veronese, Girolamo da Santacroce, Savoldo, Tintoretto.

VICTORIA AND ALBERT MUSEUM: Jacopo Bassano, Carlo Crivelli, Vittorio Crivelli, Mazzola, Tintoretto, Zelotti.

WALLACE COLLECTION: Bartolomeo Veneto, Cima, Carlo Crivelli, Titian.

BURLINGTON HOUSE: Palma Vecchio.

WESTMINSTER ABBEY: Bartolomeo Vivarini.

WESTMINSTER CATHEDRAL: Bartolomeo Montagna.

WESTMINSTER HOSPITAL: Paolo Veronese.

MERCHANT TAYLORS' COMPANY: Bordone.

BUCKINGHAM PALACE, ROYAL COLLECTION: Licinio, Mazzola.

SIR THOMAS BARLOW: Bordone.

LADY BELPER (EX): Diana.

MR. GUY BENSON: Caprioli.

MR. REX BENSON: Lotto.

R. H. BENSON COLLECTION (EX): Basaiti, Leandro Bassano, Bello, Bissolo, Cariani, Carrari da Forlì, Vittorio Crivelli, Giorgione Copies, Giorgionesque Paintings, Palma Vecchio.

LT.-COL. BROCKLEBANK: Antonio Maria da Carpi.

DUKE OF BUCCLEUCH: Pordenone.

MR. CHARLES BUTLER (EX): Catena, Carlo Crivelli, Palma Vecchio.

MR. J. P. CARRINGTON (EX): Follower of Giovanni Bellini.

HON. G. A. F. CAVENDISH BENTINCK (EX): Bonifazio Veronese, Bordone, Busati, Giovanni and Bernardino da Asola.

MR. H. M. CLARK (EX): Antonio Vivarini.

LADY CLIVE (EX): Bordone.

CORNWALLIS-WEST COLLECTION (EX): Verla.

EARL OF CRAWFORD see **Balcarres.**

COL. F. J. DAVIES: Paolo Veronese.

LORD DESBOROUGH (EX): Titian.

MR. WALTER E. TOWER (EX): Bastiani.

LORD VERNON (EX): Catena.

DUKE OF WESTMINSTER (EX): Giovanni Bellini, Lotto.

MR. W. H. WOODWARD (EX) (check): Catena, Girolamo da Santacroce, Paris Bordone.

Longana (Forlì). S. APOLLINARE: Carrari da Forlì.

Longford Castle (Salisbury, Wilts.). EARL OF RADNOR: Bordone (ex), Sebastiano del Piombo.

Longleat (Wilts.). MARQUESS OF BATH: Leandro Bassano, Bonifazio Veronese, Mocetto, Polidoro, Andrea Schiavone, Tintoretto, Titian.

Lonigo (Vicenza). SS. FERMO E RUSTICO: Montemezzano.

PIEVE DEI SS. QUIRICO E GIULITTA: Benedetto Montagna.

Lopud (Isola di Mezzo, Dubrovnik). CATTEDRALE: Campagnola.

Loreto. PALAZZO APOSTOLICO: Antonio da Faenza, Lotto.

Los Angeles (California). COUNTY MUSEUM: Bonifazio Veronese, Bordone, Dario da Treviso, Ingannati, Marconi, Paolo Veneziano, Paolo Veronese, Titian.

Los Olivos (California). MR. FRANCIS M. SEDGWICK: Follower of Giovanni Bellini.

Lovere (Brescia). GALLERIA TADINI: Bastiani, Beccaruzzi, Jacopo Bellini, Bordone, Giovanni da Bologna, Girolamo da Treviso, Ingannati, Lotto, Mocetto.

Lübeck. KATHARINENKIRCHE: Tintoretto.

Lucca. PINACOTECA: Bordone, Licinio, Polidoro, Tintoretto.

ISTITUTO D'ARTE PASSAGLIA: Paolo Veronese.

S. MARTINO (DUOMO): Tintoretto.

Lucera (Foggia). DUOMO: Girolamo da Santacroce.

Lugano. ROHONCZ COLLECTION: Agostini, Andrea da Murano, Bartolomeo Veneto, Jacopo Bassano, Bastiani (ex), Giovanni Bellini, Bordone, Vittore Carpaccio, Vittorio Crivelli, Diana, Mazzola, Montagnana, Palma Vecchio, Paolo Veneziano, Paolo Veronese, Sebastiano del Piombo, Semitecolo, Tintoretto, Titian, Bartolomeo Vivarini.

Lussingrande (Istria). CHIESA PARROCCHIALE: Bartolomeo Vivarini.

Luton Hoo (Beds.). WERNHER COLLECTION: Titian, Antonio Vivarini.

Lützschena (Leipzig). SPECK VON STERNBURG COLLECTION (EX): Cima.

Luvigliano (Padua). S. MARTINO: Girolamo da Santacroce.

Lyons. MUSÉE DES BEAUX-ARTS: Bartolomeo Montagna, Palma Vecchio, Paolo Veronese, Tintoretto.

Macerata. PINACOTECA CIVICA: Carlo Crivelli.

ORATORIO DELLA SS. TRINITÀ: Antonio Solario.

S. MARIA DELLE VERGINI: Tintoretto.

Macon (Georgia). WESLEYAN COLLEGE: Cima.

Madrid. PRADO: Basaiti, Jacopo Bassano, Leandro Bassano, Giovanni Bellini, Catena, Giorgione, Licinio, Lotto, Montemezzano, Paolo Veronese, Sebastiano del Piombo, Tintoretto, Titian.

MUSEO CERRALBO: Tintoretto.

ACADEMIA DE SAN FERNANDO: Leandro Bassano, Giovanni Bellini.

HEIRS OF DUKE OF ALBA: Palma Vecchio, Titian.

Magdeburg. KAISER-FRIEDRICH-MUSEUM: Andrea Schiavone.

Maidenhead (Berks.). SIR THOMAS MERTON: Bartolomeo Montagna.

Mainz. SCHLOSS, GEMÄLDESAMMLUNG: Marziale.

Malcontenta (Venice). VILLA FOSCARI: Zelotti.

Malpaga (Bergamo). CASTELLO COLLEONI: Fogolino.

Manchester (New Hampshire). CURRIER GALLERY OF ART: Tintoretto.

Manhasset (New York). MRS. NICHOLAS BRADY (EX): Cima.

Maniago (Udine). DUOMO: Amalteo.

Mantua. PALAZZO DUCALE (REGGIA DEI GONZAGA): Jacopo Bassano, Francesco da Milano, Tintoretto.

Marostica (Bassano del Grappa): S. ANTONIO: Jacopo Bassano.

Marseilles. MUSÉE DE LONGCHAMP: Jacopo Bassano, Cariani, Andrea Schiavone.

Masèr (Treviso). VILLA BARBARO, CONTE E CONTESSA LULING BOSCHETTI: Jacopo de' Barbari, Paolo Veronese.

Massa Fermana (Ascoli). CONFRATERNITA DELL'IMMACOLATA: Vittorio Crivelli.
MUNICIPIO: Carlo Crivelli.

Massignano (Ascoli). MUNICIPIO: Vittorio Crivelli.

Matelica (Macerata). MUSEO PIERSANTI: Jacopo Bellini, Venetian fifteenth-century unidentified.

Matera. S. FRANCESCO: Bartolomeo Vivarini.

Meano (Belluno). ORATORIO DI S. BARTOLOMEO: Mariscalchi.

Medole (Mantua). CHIESA PARROCCHIALE: Titian.

Mel (Belluno). CHIESA ARCIPRETALE: Giovanni da Mel, Mariscalchi, Andrea Schiavone.
ORATORIO DELL'ADDOLORATA: Andrea Schiavone.

Melbourne. NATIONAL GALLERY OF VICTORIA: Jacopo Bassano, Paolo Veneziano, Paolo Veronese, Tintoretto, Titian, Antonio Vivarini.

Mellerstain (Scotland). EARL OF HADDINGTON (EX): Palma Vecchio.

Mells (Somerset). MRS. RAYMOND ASQUITH: Bordone (ex), Cima, Andrea Schiavone.

Mentmore (Bucks.). COUNTESS OF ROSEBERY: Bartolomeo Veneto.
EARL OF ROSEBERY (EX): Bordone, Paolo Veronese, Tintoretto.

Merion (Pennsylvania). BARNES FOUNDATION: Bonifazio Veronese, Titian.

Mertoun House (St. Boswell's, Scotland). EARL OF ELLESMERE: Bonifazio Veronese, Bordone, Tintoretto. (See also **Edinburgh**.)

Messina. MUSEO NAZIONALE: Antonello da Messina, Antonello de Saliba, Catena.

Mexico City. F. MEYER COLLECTION: Lotto.

Mezzoldo (Bergamo). S. GIOVANNI BATTISTA: Lattanzio da Rimini.

Miglionico (Matera). EX-CONVENTO DELLA CROCIFISSIONE: Cima.

Milan. PINACOTECA DI BRERA: Alamanno, Bartolomeo Veneto, Basaiti, Jacopo Bassano, Leandro Bassano, Bastiani, Gentile Bellini, Giovanni Bellini, Jacopo Bellini, Bonifazio Veronese, Bordone, Cariani, Vittore Carpaccio, Carrari da Forlì, Cima, Carlo Crivelli, Vittorio Crivelli, Giovanni da Bologna, Girolamo da Treviso, Ingannati, Licinio, Lotto, Mansueti, Giovanni Martini da Udine, Mazzola, Bartolomeo Montagna, Benedetto Montagna, Nicola di Maestro Antonio d'Ancona, Palma Vecchio, Paolo Veneziano, Paolo Veronese, Pordenone, Previtali, Rondinelli, Girolamo da Santacroce, Savoldo, Andrea Schiavone, Speranza, Sustris, Tintoretto, Titian, Verla, Alvise Vivarini, Antonio Vivarini.

MUSEO POLDI PEZZOLI: Bastiani, Giovanni Bellini, Jacopo Bellini, Bonifazio Veronese, Cariani, Vittore Carpaccio, Cima, Carlo Crivelli, Fogolino, Lotto, Mazzola, Bartolomeo Montagna, Palma Vecchio, Previtali, Girolamo da Santacroce, Antonio Vivarini, Venetian fifteenth-century unidentified.

MUSEI CIVICI DEL CASTELLO SFORZESCO. Antonello da Messina, Leandro Bassano, Beccaruzzi, Giovanni Bellini, Bissolo, Bonifazio Veronese, Cariani, Carlo Crivelli, Licinio,

Lorenzo Veneziano, Lotto, Marconi, Bartolomeo Montagna, Girolamo da Santacroce, Andrea Schiavone, Sebastiano del Piombo, Antonio Solario, Sustris, Tintoretto, Antonio Vivarini.

PINACOTECA AMBROSIANA: Antonello de Saliba, Bartolomeo Veneto, Basaiti, Jacopo Bassano, Bonifazio Veronese, Cariani, Cima, Giovanni and Bernardino da Asola, Andrea Schiavone, Antonio Solario, Titian, Bartolomeo Vivarini.

MUSEO DEL DUOMO: Tintoretto.

PALAZZO ARCIVESCOVILE: Fogolino.

S. MARIA ALLA PORTA: Agostini.

S. MARIA PRESSO S. CELSO: Bordone.

CONTE ALDRIGHETTO CASTELBARCO ALBANI: Savoldo.

BARONE BAGATTI-VALSECCHI: Giovanni Bellini.

BIANDRÀ COLLECTION: Lotto.

BONONA CEREDA COLLECTION (EX): Previtali.

PRINCIPE BORROMEO: Bartolomeo Veneto, Gentile Bellini, Mazzola.

BRIVIO COLLECTION: Nicola di Maestro Antonio d'Ancona.

CAGNOLA COLLECTION see **Gazzada.**

CHIESA COLLECTION (EX): Montagnana.

SIG. ACHILLE COLOGNA (EX): Bartolomeo Montagna.

CRESPI COLLECTION (EX): Basaiti, Bordone, Lotto, Mansueti.

CRESPI-MORBIO COLLECTION: Savoldo.

DOTT. ALDO CRESPI: Bartolomeo Veneto, Paolo Veneziano.

COMM. MARIO CRESPI: Lotto, Antonio Vivarini.

FELTRINELLI COLLECTION: Antonello da Messina.

SIG. GIULIO FERRARIO: Filippo da Verona, Tintoretto, Francesco Vecellio.

MARCHESE FOSSATI (EX): Bartolomeo Veneto.

FRIZZONI COLLECTION (EX): Licinio, Previtali.

SIG. FRUA DE ANGELI: Tintoretto.

DUCA GALLARATI SCOTTI: Licinio.

CONTE PAOLO GERLI: Bartolomeo Veneto, Cima, Giorgionesque Furniture Painters.

GIOVIO COLLECTION (EX): Caprioli.

GNECCHI COLLECTION (EX): Giovanni Bellini.

SIG. ANTONIO GRANDI (EX): Bartolomeo Montagna.

AVV. PIETRO GUSSALLI: Savoldo.

CONTE MELZI D'ERIL: Sustris.

MELZI COLLECTION (EX): Bartolomeo Veneto.

OROMBELLI COLLECTION: Belliniano.

SIG. UMBERTO PINI (EX): Tintoretto.

SIG. VINCENZO POLLI: Catena.

PRINETTI COLLLECTION (EX): Giovanni Bellini.

RASINI COLLECTION: Paolo Veronese.

SAIBENE COLLECTION: Belliniano, Giambono, Previtali, Tintoretto.

SPERONI COLLECTION: Antonio Vivarini.

SIG. OTTAVIANO VENIER: Lotto, Polidoro, Andrea Schiavone, Tintoretto.

CONTE G. P. VENINO: Bartolomeo Veneto.

Milazzo (Messina). CHIESA MADRE: Antonello de Saliba.

Minneapolis (Minnesota). INSTITUTE OF ARTS: Antonio Maria da Carpi, Basaiti, Jacopo Bassano, Palma Vecchio, Paolo Veronese, Girolamo da Santacroce, Tintoretto, Titian, Verla.

MR. JOHN R. VANDERLIP (EX): Simone da Cusighe.

Modena. GALLERIA ESTENSE: Antonello da Messina, Jacopo Bassano, Bonifazio Veronese, Cariani, Catena, Cima, Diana, Mansueti, Marconi, Mazzola, Mocetto, Bartolomeo Montagna, Paolo Veronese, Girolamo da Santacroce.

S. PIETRO: Girolamo di Tommaso da Treviso.

Mogliano (Macerata). CHIESA PARROCCHIALE: Lotto.

Monaco. PRINCE OF MONACO: Titian.

Monopoli (Bari). PALAZZO DEL COMUNE: Paolo Veronese.

DUOMO: Bastiani.

S. ANGELO: Follower of Giovanni Bellini.

S. ANTONIO: Follower of Giovanni Bellini.

S. LEONARDO: Polidoro.

Monselice (Padua). CONTE VITTORIO CINI: Venetian fifteenth-century unidentified.

Montagnana. MUNICIPIO: Buonconsiglio.

DUOMO: Buonconsiglio, Paolo Veronese.

Montauban. MUSÉE INGRES: Benedetto Carpaccio, Fogolino, Verla.

Montecchio Maggiore (Vicenza). S. PIETRO: Buonconsiglio.

Montefalcone Apennino (Ascoli). CHIESA CONVENTUALE DEI MINORI RIFORMATI: Alamanno.

Montefiore dell'Aso (Ascoli). S. LUCIA: Carlo Crivelli.

Montefortino (Ascoli). PINACOTECA CIVICA: Alamanno.

Montelupone (Macerata). S. FRANCESCO: Antonio da Faenza.

Monte Ortone (Padua). SANTUARIO: Montagnana.

Monte San Giusto (Macerata). S. MARIA IN TELUSIANO: Lotto.

Montesanmartino (Macerata). S. MARTINO: Carlo Crivelli, Vittorio Crivelli.

S. MARIA DEL POZZO: Vittorio Crivelli.

Montevideo. DR. K. A. BERGAMALI: Bonifazio Veronese.

Montpellier. MUSÉE FABRE: Bissolo, Paolo Veronese.

Montreal. MUSEUM OF FINE ARTS: Tintoretto.

MR. E. B. HOMER: Veneto-Byzantine Painters.

W. D. LIGHTHALL COLLECTION: Andrea Schiavone.

Morano Calabro (Cosenza). S. BERNARDINO: Bartolomeo Vivarini.

Mori (Trent). CHIESA PARROCCHIALE: Verla.

Moriago (Treviso). CHIESA PARROCCHIALE: Pordenone.

Mortegliano (Udine). CHIESA PARROCCHIALE: Giovanni Martini da Udine.

Moscow. MUSEUM OF FINE ARTS: Savoldo, Andrea Schiavone.

Motta di Livenza (Treviso). S. NICCOLÒ (DUOMO): Amalteo, Leandro Bassano.

SANTUARIO DELLA MADONNA DEI MIRACOLI: Giovanni and Bernardino da Asola, Pordenone.

SCARPA COLLECTION (EX): Mancini.

Mount Stewart (Ireland). DOWAGER MARCHIONESS OF LONDONDERRY (EX): Giovanni Bellini.

Mugnai (Belluno). CHIESA ARCIPRETALE: Mariscalchi.

Muncie (Indiana). BALL STATE TEACHERS COLLEGE: Giovanni Bellini.

Munich. ALTE PINAKOTHEK: Antonello da Messina, Antonello de Saliba, Jacopo de' Barbari, Basaiti, Jacopo Bassano, Leandro Bassano, Bordone, Cariani, Vittore Carpaccio, Cima, Filippo da Verona, Florigerio, Jacopo da Valenza, Licinio, Lotto, Marconi, Palma Vecchio, Paolo Veronese, Andrea Schiavone, Sustris, Tintoretto, Titian, Francesco Vecellio.

FLEISCHMANN COLLECTION (EX): Lotto.

HERR GEORG HIRTH (EX): Leandro Bassano.

LÖTZBECK COLLECTION: Cariani, Mazzola, Savoldo.

NEMES COLLECTION (EX): Giovanni Bellini, Caselli da Parma, Licinio.

HEIRS OF PRINCE RUPRECHT OF BAVARIA: Giovanni Bellini.

Münster. PROVINZIALMUSEUM: Follower of Vittore Carpaccio.

Murano see **Venice** (Environs).

Mussolente (Vicenza). CHIESA PARROCCHIALE: Andrea da Murano, Jacopo Bassano.

Naestved see **Copenhagen.**

Nancy. MUSÉE: Bartolomeo Veneto, Lotto, Tintoretto.

Nantes. MUSÉE DOBRÉE. Basaiti, Bordone, Polidoro, Tintoretto.

Naples. MUSEO NAZIONALE (GALLERIE NAZIONALI DI CAPODIMONTE): Antonello da Messina, Jac . . . Bar . . . , Leandro Bassano, Giovanni Bellini, Caselli da Parma, Lotto, Mazzola, Palma Vecchio, Pordenone, Girolamo da Santacroce, Andrea Schiavone, Sebastiano del Piombo, Antonio Solario, Titian, Alvise Vivarini, Bartolomeo Vivarini.

MUSEO FILANGIERI: Pordenone.

S. DOMENICO MAGGIORE: Titian.

CERTOSA DI SAN MARTINO: Paolo Veronese.

S. RESTITUTA: Antonio Solario.

CHIOSTRO DEI SS. SEVERINO E SOSIO: Antonio Solario.

Narbonne. MUSÉE: Tintoretto.

Nembro (Bergamo). S. NICOLA: Gavazzi.

S. SEBASTIANO: Gavazzi.

Neuwied. SCHLOSS SEGENHAUS. FÜRST ZU WIED (EX): Marziale.

Newark (New Jersey). MUSEUM: Bastiani.

New Haven (Conn.). YALE UNIVERSITY: Giovanni Bellini, Bonifazio Veronese, Carlo Crivelli, Vittorio Crivelli, Florigerio, Francesco de' Franceschi, Giorgione, Ingannati, Paolo Veneziano, Girolamo da Santacroce, Tintoretto, Verla, Bartolomeo Vivarini. (Numbers beginning with 1871 refer to pictures of the Jarves Collection.)

New Orleans (Louisiana). I. DELGADO MUSEUM OF ART: Agostini, Vittore Carpaccio, Ingannati, Lotto, Paolo Veronese, Tintoretto, Bartolomeo Vivarini.

Newport (Rhode Island). MR. WALTER COLES CABALL: Tintoretto.

MRS. DUKE: Palma Vecchio.

New York. METROPOLITAN MUSEUM OF ART: Antonello da Messina, Antonello de Saliba, Jacopo de' Barbari, Bartolomeo Veneto, Jacopo Bassano, Leandro Bassano, Giovanni Bellini, Bonifazio Veronese, Bragadin, Vittore Carpaccio, Caselli da Parma, Catena, Cima, Carlo Crivelli, Vittorio Crivelli, Giambono, Giorgione, Licinio, Lotto, Bartolomeo Montagna, Niccolò di Pietro, Paolo Veronese, Savoldo, Sebastiano del Piombo, Tintoretto, Titian, Antonio Vivarini, Bartolomeo Vivarini, Venetian fifteenth-century unidentified.

FRICK COLLECTION: Jacopo Bassano, Bastiani, Gentile Bellini, Giovanni Bellini, Paolo Veneziano, Paolo Veronese, Titian.

HISTORICAL SOCIETY: Bordone.

S. H. KRESS FOUNDATION: Agostini, Antonello de Saliba, Jacopo de' Barbari, Bartolomeo Veneto, Basaiti, Jacopo Bassano, Leandro Bassano, Bastiani, Giovanni Bellini, Bonifazio Veronese, Bordone, Campagnola, Cariani, Vittore Carpaccio, Catena, Cima, Carlo Crivelli, Vittorio Crivelli, Diana, Duia, Gavazzi, Giorgionesque Paintings, Girolamo di Tommaso da Treviso, Grassi, Ingannati, Jacopo da Valenza, Lattanzio da Rimini,

Licinio, Lorenzo Veneziano, Lotto, Marconi, Bartolomeo Montagna, Palma Vecchio, Paolo Veneziano, Paolo Veronese, Pordenone, Previtali, Girolamo da Santacroce, Savoldo, Sebastiano del Piombo, Tintoretto, Titian, Bartolomeo Vivarini.

PIERPONT MORGAN LIBRARY: Giovanni Bellini, Cima, Tintoretto.

MOGMAR FOUNDATION: Lotto.

ST. BONAVENTURE'S SCHOOL: Giovanni Bellini.

CATHEDRAL OF S. JOHN THE DIVINE: Paolo Veronese.

MR. MAX ASCOLI: Tintoretto.

MR. R. AUSPITZER: Catena.

MR. JULES BACHE (EX): Giorgione.

MR. FRANCIS L. BACON: Antonio Vivarini.

MR. EUGENE BOROSS: Licinio.

MR. WALTER P. CHRYSLER JR.: Bonifazio Veronese, Vittorio Crivelli, Mariscalchi, Paolo Veronese, Andrea Schiavone, Sustris, Tintoretto.

MR. JOHN ROSS DELAFIELD: Tintoretto.

DREICER COLLECTION (EX): Girolamo da Vicenza.

MRS. A. W. ERICKSON: Carlo Crivelli.

JUDGE GARY (EX): Tintoretto.

MR. C. GRIVAKIS (EX): Jacobello del Fiore.

HORACE HARDING'S HEIRS: Sebastiano del Piombo.

W. R. HEARST COLLECTION (EX): Lotto, Girolamo da Santacroce.

MR. AND MRS. CHARLES V. HICKOX: Giovanni Bellini, Cima, Paolo Veronese (Paolo Veneziano on loan to Chicago), Titian.

F. MARTIN JOSEPH COLLECTION: Lotto.

MR. L. R. KAUFMANN: Licinio.

MRS. ARTHUR LEHMAN: Carlo Crivelli, Bartolomeo Vivarini.

PHILIP AND ROBERT LEHMAN COLLECTION: Giovanni Bellini, Carlo Crivelli, Lorenzo Veneziano, Tintoretto, Bartolomeo Vivarini.

MR. E. D. LEVINSON (EX): Bartolomeo Veneto.

BERTINA AND ROBERT MANNING: Bordone, Paolo Veronese, Sebastiano del Piombo.

MR. MCKINNON: Licinio.

MRS. ROBERT MINTURN (EX): Vittore Carpaccio.

MR. CLARENCE Y. PALITZ: Pennacchi.

PULITZER COLLECTION (EX): Caprioli.

MR. WILLIAM SALOMON (EX): Catena.

MR. LEON SCHINASI (EX): Bartolomeo Veneto, Catena.

DR. JOHN E. STILWELL (EX): Cariani.

MR. OSCAR STRAUSS: Cariani.

MRS. RUTHERFORD STUYVESANT (EX): Oliverio.

DR. W. SUIDA: Jacopo Bassano, Bonifazio Veronese, Licinio, Paolo Veronese, Andrea Schiavone, Alvise Vivarini.

MR. MYRON TAYLOR: Oliverio.

MR. BOYCE THOMPSON (EX): Bordone.

MRS. JULIUS WEITZNER: Bonifazio Veronese, Polidoro.

HOWARD YOUNG (EX): Tintoretto.

Nîmes. MUSÉE DES BEAUX-ARTS: Bartolomeo Veneto, Jacopo Bassano, Giambono.

Nivaagard (Copenhagen). HAGE COLLECTION: Giovanni Bellini, Bonifazio Veronese, Bordone, Cima, Lattanzio da Rimini, Lotto, Francesco da Santacroce, Titian.

Noale (Padua). CHIESA PARROCCHIALE: Lattanzio da Rimini.

Norcia. S. BENEDETTO: Antonio da Faenza.

Northampton see **Castle Ashby** and **Compton Wynyates.**

North Mimms (Herts.). MRS. WALTER BURNS: Jacopo Bellini.

Northwick Park (Blockley, Worcs.). CAPTAIN SPENCER CHURCHILL: Bonifazio Veronese, Bordone, Cariani.

Norton Hall (Glos.). MRS. W. M. H. POLLEN: Palma Vecchio, Francesco da Santacroce.

Nuneham Park (Oxford). VISCOUNT HARCOURT: Gentile Bellini.

Oderzo (Treviso). S. GIOVANNI BATTISTA (formerly DUOMO): Amalteo.
SCUOLA DELLA CONFRATERNITA: Amalteo.

Offida (Ascoli). MUNICIPIO: Alamanno.

Olantigh Towers (Wye, Kent). MR. SAWBRIDGE ERLE-DRAX (EX): Giovanni Bellini, Palma Vecchio.

Oldenburg. AUGUSTEUM (EX): Giorgione Copies, Previtali, Sebastiano del Piombo.

Olera (Bergamo). CHIESA PARROCCHIALE: Cima.

Oliero di Valstagna (Vicenza). CHIESA PARROCCHIALE: Francesco Bassano the Elder.

Omaha (Nebraska). JOSLYN MEMORIAL ART MUSEUM: Mansueti, Marziale, Andrea Solario, Titian.

Onara (Padua). CHIESA PARROCCHIALE: Jacopo Bassano.

Oneta (Bergamo). SANTUARIO: Girolamo da Santacroce.

Orgiano (Vicenza). CHIESA PARROCCHIALE: Bartolomeo Montagna.

Oriago sul Brenta. CHIESA PARROCCHIALE: Francesco Vecellio.

Orleans. MUSÉE DE L'HÔTEL DE VILLE: Tintoretto.

Osigo (Treviso). CHIESA PARROCCHIALE: Francesco da Milano.

Osimo (Ancona). PALAZZO COMUNALE: Lotto (EX), Antonio Vivarini, Bartolomeo Vivarini.
S. GIUSEPPE DA COPERTINO: Antonio Solario.

Oslo. NATIONAL GALLERY: Jacopo Bassano, Bordone, Cariani.

Osoppo (Udine). CHIESA PARROCCHIALE: Pellegrino da San Daniele.

Ostuni (Brindisi). SS. ANNUNZIATA: Paolo Veronese.

Ottawa. NATIONAL GALLERY OF CANADA: Giovanni Bellini, Bello, Cariani, Bartolomeo Montagna, Palma Vecchio, Paolo Veronese, Tintoretto.

Otterlo (Holland). RIJKSMUSEUM: Tintoretto.

Oxford. ASHMOLEAN MUSEUM: Jacopo Bassano, Leandro Bassano, Giovanni Bellini, Bonifazio Veronese, Cariani, Carlo Crivelli, Vittorio Crivelli, Francesco dei Franceschi, Girolamo di Tommaso da Treviso, Licinio, Mocetto, Bartolomeo Montagna, Nicola di Maestro Antonio d'Ancona, Palma Vecchio, Paolo Veronese, Sustris, Tintoretto.
CHRIST CHURCH LIBRARY: Bello, Lotto, Montagnana, Montemezzano, Previtali, Andrea Schiavone, Sustris, Tintoretto, Titian.
NEW COLLEGE: Speranza.
REV. COOK (EX): Bonifazio Veronese.

Padua. MUSEO CIVICO: Agapiti, Niccolò de' Barbari, Bartolomeo Veneto, Basaiti, Jacopo Bassano, Leandro Bassano, Bastiani, Beccaruzzi, Gentile Bellini, Giovanni Bellini, Follower of Giovanni Bellini, Jacopo Bellini, Bissolo, Bonifazio Veronese, Bordone, Buonconsiglio, Campagnola, Cima, Filippo da Verona, Florigerio, Francesco de' Franceschi, Giambono, Giorgionesque Furniture Painters, Giovanni da Bologna, Giovanni and Bernardino da Asola, Girolamo da Treviso, Girolamo da Udine, Jacopo da Valenza, Licinio, Lorenzo Veneziano, Mansueti, Mazzola, Montagnana, Morto da Feltre, Paolo Veronese, Pennacchi, Pietro da Messina, Previtali, Francesco da Santacroce, Girolamo da Santacroce, Andrea Schiavone, Tintoretto, Verla, Vincenzo dalle Destre, Alvise Vivarini, Bartolomeo Vivarini.

BIBLIOTECA CAPITOLARE: Semitecolo.

PALAZZO DONDI DALL'OROLOGIO: Campagnola.

PALAZZO INDRI: Campagnola.

PALAZZO LIVIANO: Titian.

PALAZZO SELVATICO: Campagnola.

PALAZZO VESCOVILE: Bartolomeo Montagna, Montagnana.

CASA DEL CLERO: Paolo Veneziano.

ASSUNTA (DUOMO): Follower of Gentile Bellini, Marconi, Montagnana, Paris Bordone.

SS. FILIPPO E GIACOMO (EREMITANI): Fogolino, Semitecolo, Antonio Vivarini.

S. ANTONIO (BASILICA DEL SANTO): Follower of Giovanni Bellini, Filippo da Verona, Giovanni and Bernardino da Asola, Montagnana.

S. CROCE: Campagnola.

S. GIUSTINA: Campagnola, Paolo Veronese.

IMMACOLATA: Bonifazio Veronese.

S. MARIA DEI SERVI: Montagnana.

S. MARIA IN VANZO: Jacopo Bassano, Bartolomeo Montagna, Sustris.

S. NICCOLÒ: Montagnana.

S. TOMMASO DEI FILIPPINI: Antonio Vivarini.

ORATORIO DI S. BOVO: Florigerio.

SCUOLA DEL CARMINE: Campagnola.

SCUOLA DI S. ROCCO: Campagnola.

SCUOLA DI S. ANTONIO (DEL SANTO): Campagnola, Filippo da Verona, Bartolomeo Montagna, Benedetto Montagna, Titian.

CONTE NOVELLO PAPAFAVA: Leandro Bassano, Campagnola, Giovanni and Bernardino da Asola, Marconi, Bartolomeo Montagna.

Paese (Treviso). CHIESA PARROCCHIALE: Girolamo da Treviso.

Paggese di Acquasanta (Ascoli). S. LORENZO: Alamanno.

Pagliara (Messina). S. SEBASTIANO: Antonello de Saliba.

Palermo. GALLERIA NAZIONALE DI SICILIA: Antonello da Messina, Antonello de Saliba, Basaiti, Jacopo Bassano.

CHIARAMONTE BORDONARO COLLECTION: Bissolo, Girolamo da Santacroce.

VIRZI COLLECTION (EX): Sebastiano del Piombo.

Paola (Cosenza). SANTUARIO DI S. FRANCESCO: Antonello de Saliba.

Parcieux (Lyons). CHALANDON COLLECTION (EX): Bastiani, Mansueti.

Parenzo (Istria). DUOMO: Antonio Vivarini.

Paris. MUSÉES DU LOUVRE: Antonello da Messina, Jacopo de' Barbari, Bartolomeo Veneto, Jacopo Bassano, Leandro Bassano, Follower of Gentile Bellini, Giovanni Bellini, Jacopo Bellini, Bonifazio Veronese, Bordone, Cariani, Vittore Carpaccio, Catena, Cima, Carlo Crivelli, Giorgione, Licinio, Lorenzo Veneziano, Lotto, Mancini, Marziale, Bartolomeo Montagna, Montemezzano, Palma Vecchio, Paolo Veneziano, Paolo Veronese, Polidoro, Savoldo, Andrea Schiavone, Sebastiano del Piombo, Sustris, Tintoretto, Titian, Alvise Vivarini, Antonio Vivarini, Bartolomeo Vivarini, Venetian fifteenth-century unidentified.

MUSÉES NATIONAUX, CAMPANA COLLECTION: Basaiti, Cima, Carlo Crivelli, Vittorio

Crivelli, Grassi, Marconi, Paolo Veneziano, Rondinelli, Antonio Vivarini, Zannino di Pietro.

MUSÉE JACQUEMART-ANDRÉ: Antonello de Saliba, Bastiani, Giovanni Bellini, Vittore Carpaccio, Catena, Cima, Carlo Crivelli, Vittorio Crivelli, Girolamo da Vicenza, Licinio, Montemezzano, Palma Vecchio, Rosso, Girolamo da Santacroce, Francesco Vecellio, Bartolomeo Vivarini.

PETIT PALAIS: Cima.

S. ÉTIENNE DU MONT: Girolamo da Santacroce.

S. FRANÇOIS XAVIER: Tintoretto.

S. HONORÉ D'EYLAU: Tintoretto.

S. LOUIS EN L'ILE: Follower of Giovanni Bellini, Giovanni and Bernardino da Asola.

PRINCESS ALTIORA-COLONNA (EX): Benedetto Carpaccio.

M. AYNARD (EX): Cariani.

DELAROFF COLLECTION (EX): Basaiti, Boldrini, Jacobello di Antonello.

DOLLFUS COLLECTION: Paolo Veneziano.

DUVAL FOULC: Alamanno.

MME. FRANGHY: Palma Vecchio.

MARQUIS DE GANAY: Giorgionesque Furniture Painters, Titian.

HEUGEL COLLECTION: Bartolomeo Veneto, Bordone, Lotto, Mazzola.

MARTIN LE ROY COLLECTION (EX): Giovanni Bellini.

M. LINET: Stefano di Sant'Agnese.

GASTON MENIER (EX): Tintoretto.

VICOMTESSE DE NOAILLES: Bartolomeo Montagna.

FERNANDO PEREZ COLLECTION (EX): Bastiani.

COMTE DE POURTALÈS (EX): Giovanni Bellini.

BARONNE EDOUARD DE ROTHSCHILD: Palma Vecchio, Sebastiano del Piombo.

BARON MAURICE DE ROTHSCHILD (EX): Bartolomeo Veneto.

MAX ROTHSCHILD (EX): Girolamo da Santacroce.

MR. ARTHUR SACHS: Giorgione.

COMTESSE SALA (MRS. E. BAYER): Previtali.

SAMBON COLLECTION: Paolo Veronese.

E. J. SARTORIS (EX): Alamanno.

ADOLPHE SCHLOSS COLLECTION (EX): Catena.

MRS. STANDISH (EX): Follower of Vittore Carpaccio.

DUC DE TRÉVISE (EX): Pennacchi.

Parma. REGIA GALLERIA: Bartolomeo Veneto, Caselli da Parma, Cima, Mazzola, Mocetto, Paolo Veneziano, Andrea Schiavone, Sebastiano del Piombo.

DUOMO: Caselli da Parma, Mazzola, Girolamo da Santacroce.

S. GIOVANNI EVANGELISTA: Caselli da Parma.

Partenkirchen (Bavaria). WIGGER COLLECTION (EX): Lotto.

Patti (Messina). DUOMO: Antonello de Saliba.

Pau. MUSÉE: Tintoretto.

Pavia. GALLERIA MALASPINA: Antonello da Messina, Giovanni Bellini, Diana, Giambono, Jacobello del Fiore, Licinio, Mansueti, Mocetto.

(Environs). CERTOSA, MUSEO: Bartolomeo Montagna.

Pedavena (Belluno). CHIESA PARROCCHIALE: Mariscalchi.

Peghera (Bergamo). CHIESA PARROCCHIALE: Palma Vecchio.

Perarolo (Belluno). S. ROCCO: Francesco Vecellio.

Perth (W. Australia). MUSEUM: Jacopo Bassano, Tintoretto.

Perugia. PINACOTECA VANNUCCI: Ingannati, Girolamo da Santacroce.

Pesaro. MUSEI CIVICI. Giovanni Bellini, Jacobello del Fiore, Niccolò di Pietro.
  MUSEO MOSCA: Mansueti.

Petworth (Sussex). NATIONAL TRUST: Bonifazio Veronese, Titian.

Philadelphia (Pennsylvania). JOHN G. JOHNSON COLLECTION: Antonello da Messina,
  Antonello de Saliba, Jacopo de' Barbari, Basaiti, Leandro Bassano, Bastiani, Follower
  of Gentile Bellini, Giovanni Bellini, Bordone, Campagnola, Cariani, Vittore Carpaccio,
  Catena, Cima, Carlo Crivelli, Vittorio Crivelli, Folchetti, Licinio, Lotto, Marconi,
  Mariscalchi, Bartolomeo Montagna, Benedetto Montagna, Palma Vecchio, Paolo
  Veronese, Pordenone, Rondinelli, Girolamo da Santacroce, Sebastiano del Piombo,
  Tintoretto, Titian, Alvise Vivarini, Bartolomeo Vivarini, Venetian sixteenth-century
  unidentified.
  MUSEUM OF ART: Vittorio Crivelli, Jacobello del Fiore, Titian.
  WILSTACH COLLECTION (EX): Palma Vecchio, Tintoretto (ex).
  MR. J. MCILHENNY (EX): Giorgionesque Paintings.

Piacenza. MUSEO CIVICO: Antonello da Messina, Mazzola, Pordenone.
  MADONNA DI CAMPAGNA: Pordenone.

Pianezza (Vicenza). CHIESA PARROCCHIALE: Jacopo Bassano.

Pianiga (Venice). CHIESA PARROCCHIALE: Bissolo.

Piazzola sul Brenta (Padua). VILLA CAMERINI: Bartolomeo Veneto, Belliniano.

Pieve di Cadore (Belluno). CHIESA ARCIPRETALE: Francesco Vecellio.
  CHIESA ARCIDIACONALE: Titian.

Pieve di Soligo (Treviso). CHIESA PARROCCHIALE: Francesco da Milano.

Pinzano (Udine). S. STEFANO: Pordenone.

Piove di Sacco (Padua). MADONNA DELLE GRAZIE: Mocetto.
  S. MARTINO: Guglielmo da Venezia, Jacopo da Valenza, Paolo Veneziano, Silvio.

Pirano (Istria). PALAZZO COMUNALE: Benedetto Carpaccio.
  DUOMO: Paolo Veneziano.
  S. FRANCESCO: Vittore Carpaccio.

Pisino (Istria). S. FRANCESCO: Girolamo da Santacroce.

Pittsburgh (Pennsylvania). CARNEGIE INSTITUTE: Vittore Carpaccio.

Poggio di Bretta (Ascoli). CHIESA PARROCCHIALE: Carlo Crivelli.

Pola (Istria). MUSEO CIVICO: Vittore Carpaccio.

Polesden Lacey (Surrey). NATIONAL TRUST: Diana.

Polignano a Mare (Bari). DUOMO: Antonio Vivarini, Bartolomeo Vivarini.

Pommersfelden (Bamberg). SCHÖNBORN COLLECTION: Titian.

Ponte a Moriano (Lucca). EDITA VON ZUR MUEHLEN (EX): Paolo Veronese.

Ponteranica (Bergamo). SS. VINCENZO ED ALESSANDRO: Cariani, Lotto.

Pordenone. PALAZZO COMUNALE: Pordenone.
  S. MARCO (DUOMO): Amalteo, Fogolino, Pordenone.

Portland (Oregon). ART MUSEUM: Bastiani, Giovanni Bellini, Carlo Crivelli, Girolamo da
  Treviso, Ingannati.

Portogruaro (Treviso). DUOMO: Amalteo, Giovanni Martini da Udine.
  S. LUIGI: Amalteo.

Port Washington (New York). S. GUGGENHEIM COLLECTION: Vittore Carpaccio.

Posen. MUSEUM: Jacopo Bassano, Bonifazio Veronese, Catena, Palma Vecchio, Polidoro.
  RACZYNSKI COLLECTION (EX): Mazzola.

Potsdam. SANSSOUCI: Licinio.

Poughkeepsie (New York). VASSAR COLLEGE: Tintoretto, Antonio Vivarini, Bartolomeo Vivarini.

Pove del Grappa (Vicenza). CHIESA PARROCCHIALE: Jacopo Bassano.

Povo (Trent). CHIESA PARROCCHIALE: Fogolino.

Pozzale di Cadore (Belluno). CHIESA PARROCCHIALE: Vittore Carpaccio.

Praglia (Padua). MONASTERO (BADIA): Bartolomeo Montagna, Zelotti.

     S. MARIA ASSUNTA: Zelotti.

Prague. NATIONAL GALLERY: Leandro Bassano, Bordone, Catena, Lorenzo Veneziano, Palma Vecchio, Girolamo da Santacroce, Antonio Vivarini.

Pratolino see **Florence** (Environs).

Princeton (New Jersey). UNIVERSITY GALLERY: Andrea da Murano, Jac ... Bar ... , Jacopo Bassano, Diana, Giorgione Copies, Lotto, Mocetto, Paolo Veronese, Girolamo da Santacroce, Andrea Schiavone, Antonio Solario, Tintoretto, Antonio Vivarini.

     MRS. FRANK J. MATHER: Pordenone.

     F. J. MATHER COLLECTION (EX): Diana, Andrea Schiavone.

Prodolone (Udine). S. MARIA DELLE GRAZIE: Amalteo.

Provesano (Udine). CHIESA PARROCCHIALE: Gianfrancesco da Tolmezzo.

Providence (Rhode Island). RHODE ISLAND SCHOOL OF DESIGN: Basaiti, Jacopo Bassano, Previtali, Tintoretto.

Puckle Hill (Kent). EARL OF DARNLEY (EX): Palma Vecchio.

Quero (Feltre). CHIESA PARROCCHIALE: Jacopo Bassano.

Ragusa (Sicily). AREZZO COLLECTION: Antonello de Saliba.

Ragusa (Dalmatia) see **Dubrovnik.**

Raleigh (North Carolina). ART MUSEUM: Jacopo Bassano, Bordone, Cima.

Randazzo (Calabria). S. NICOLA: Antonello de Saliba.

Ranica (Bergamo). CHIESA PARROCCHIALE: Bartolomeo Vivarini.

Ravenna. ACCADEMIA: Antonio Maria da Carpi, Bordone, Carrari da Forlì, Fogolino, Ingannati, Bartolomeo Montagna, Rondinelli, Antonio Vivarini, Venetian fifteenth-century unidentified.

     DUOMO: Rondinelli.

     S. DOMENICO: Rondinelli.

     CASA NADIANI-MONALDINI (EX): Rondinelli.

Recanati (Macerata). PINACOTECA COMUNALE: Lotto.

     CATTEDRALE: Folchetti.

     S. DOMENICO: Lotto.

     S. MARIA DI CASTELNUOVO: Guglielmo da Venezia.

     S. MARIA DEI MERCANTI: Lotto.

     CONTE LEOPARDI: Lotto.

Reggio Calabria. MUSEO DELLA MAGNA GRECIA: Antonello da Messina.

Rennes. MUSÉE DES BEAUX-ARTS: Jacopo Bassano, Paolo Veronese.

Rheims. MUSÉE DES BEAUX-ARTS: Carrari da Forlì, Lotto.

Richmond (Surrey). COOK COLLECTION (also EX): Antonello da Messina, Leandro Bassano, Giovanni Bellini, Cima, Giorgione, Giorgionesque Paintings, Giovanni and Bernardino da Asola, Mansueti, Marziale, Mazzola, Andrea Schiavone, Sebastiano del Piombo, Tintoretto, Titian, Francesco Vecellio.

Richmond (Virginia). MUSEUM OF FINE ARTS: Vittorio Crivelli, Tintoretto.

Rieti. PALAZZO COMUNALE: Zannino di Pietro.

Rimini. PALAZZO COMUNALE: Giovanni Bellini.

    S. FRANCESCO (TEMPIO MALATESTIANO): Francesco de Bais Imolese.

    S. GIULIANO: Paolo Veronese.

Rio de Janeiro. MACHADA COELHO COLLECTION: Tintoretto.

Ripatransone (Ascoli). MUSEO CIVICO: Vittorio Crivelli.

Rochester (New York). MR. GEORGE EASTMAN: Tintoretto.

Rome. GALLERIA BORGHESE: Antonello da Messina, Jacopo Bassano, Leandro Bassano, Giovanni Bellini, Bonifazio Veronese, Bordone, Caprioli, Cariani, Vittore Carpaccio, Follower of Vittore Carpaccio, Giorgione, Girolamo di Tommaso da Treviso, Licinio, Lotto, Mancini, Mansueti, Bartolomeo Montagna, Oliverio, Palma Vecchio, Paolo Veronese, Pordenone, Girolamo da Santacroce, Savoldo, Sebastiano del Piombo, Sustris, Titian, Bartolomeo Vivarini.

    GALLERIA COLONNA: Alamanno, Leandro Bassano, Beccaruzzi, Bonifazio Veronese, Bordone, Lotto, Palma Vecchio, Paolo Veronese, Sustris, Tintoretto, Bartolomeo Vivarini.

    GALLERIA DORIA-PAMPHILJ: Bartolomeo Veneto, Basaiti, Leandro Bassano, Beccaruzzi, Giovanni Bellini, Bonifazio Veronese, Bordone, Catena, Lotto, Paolo Veronese, Polidoro, Rondinelli, Antonio Solario, Tintoretto, Titian.

    GALLERIA NAZIONALE (PALAZZO BARBERINI): Bartolomeo Veneto, Jacopo Bassano, Cariani, Giambono, Lotto, Niccolò di Pietro, Rondinelli, Tintoretto.

    GALLERIA NAZIONALE (PALAZZO CORSINI): Bonifazio Veronese, Oliverio, Girolamo da Santacroce.

    MUSEO DI CASTEL S. ANGELO: Bordone, Carlo Crivelli, Ingannati, Lotto, Bartolomeo Montagna, Savoldo.

    MUSEO DI PALAZZO VENEZIA: Alamanno, Antonello de Saliba, Niccolò de' Barbari, Bartolomeo Veneto, Jacopo Bassano, Giovanni Bellini, Cariani, Caterino Veneziano, Francesco de' Franceschi, Licinio, Mancini, Marconi, Paolo Veneziano, Girolamo da Santacroce, Tintoretto, Titian.

    PINACOTECA CAPITOLINA: Jacopo Bassano, Leandro Bassano, Giovanni Bellini, Buonconsiglio, Duia, Lotto, Palma Vecchio, Paolo Veronese, Polidoro, Savoldo, Titian, Venetian sixteenth-century unidentified.

    PINACOTECA VATICANA: Basaiti, Giovanni Bellini, Bonifazio Veronese, Bordone, Buonconsiglio, Carrari da Forlì, Carlo Crivelli, Filippo da Verona, Bartolomeo Montagna, Nicola di Maestro Antonio d'Ancona, Niccolò di Pietro, Paolo Veronese, Sebastiano del Piombo, Titian, Antonio Vivarini, Bartolomeo Vivarini.

    ACCADEMIA DEI LINCEI: Licinio.

    ACCADEMIA DI SAN LUCA: Jacopo Bassano, Giovanni Bellini, Titian.

    FARNESINA: Sebastiano del Piombo.

    S. MARIA DEL POPOLO: Sebastiano del Piombo.

    S. PIETRO IN MONTORIO: Sebastiano del Piombo.

    PALAZZO MASSIMO ALLE COLONNE: Nicola di Maestro Antonio d'Ancona.

    PALAZZO PATRIZI (EX): Polidoro.

    PALAZZO ROSPIGLIOSI, PALLAVICINI COLLECTION: Antonello de Saliba, Lotto, Polidoro, Tintoretto.

    GALLERIA DI PALAZZO SPADA: Leandro Bassano.

    PALAZZO TAVERNA: Bonifazio Veronese.

BRITISH EMBASSY: Andrea Schiavone.

ALBERTINI COLLECTION: Bartolomeo Veneto, Lotto, Savoldo, Titian.

PRINCIPE BARBERINI (EX): Licinio, Palma Vecchio.

PRINCE BARIATINSKI (EX): Giovanni Bellini.

SENATORE RAFFAELE BASTIANELLI: Tintoretto.

CONTE NICCOLÒ CARANDINI: Paolo Veronese.

PRINCIPE CHIGI: Bonifazio Veronese, Licinio (EX).

PRINCIPE DORIA-PAMPHILJ: Jacopo Bassano, Lotto, Sebastiano del Piombo.

LAZZARONI COLLECTION (EX): Licinio, Francesco da Santacroce, Girolamo da Santacroce.

LUPI COLLECTION: Lotto.

SIGNORA ADELE DE MARIA MACCHI: Pordenone.

MENEGONI COLLECTION (EX): Mariscalchi.

ODESCALCHI-BALBI COLLECTION: Bonifazio Veronese.

PAOLO PAOLINI COLLECTION (EX): Lotto.

SIR R. RODD (EX): Palma Vecchio.

STERBINI COLLECTION (EX): Alvise Vivarini.

STROGANOFF COLLECTION (EX): Giovanni Bellini.

PROF. L. VENTURI: Giorgionesque Furniture Paintings.

MARCHESE CARLO VISCONTI VENOSTA (EX): Palma Vecchio, Rondinelli.

ZOCCA COLLECTION: Lotto.

Roncade (Treviso). CHIESA PARROCCHIALE: Bordone.

Rorai Grande. S. LORENZO: Pordenone.

Rosà (Vicenza). CHIESA PARROCCHIALE: Leandro Bassano.

CASA DI RIPOSO: Francesco Bassano.

Rossie Priory (Perthshire, Scotland). LORD KINNAIRD: Giovanni Bellini (ex), Licinio (ex), Zelotti.

Rotterdam. VAN BEUNINGEN COLLECTION see **Vierhouten.**

Rouen. MUSÉE DES BEAUX-ARTS: Girolamo di Tommaso da Treviso, Paolo Veronese.

Rovigo. ACCADEMIA DE' CONCORDI: Giovanni Bellini, Bello, Bissolo, Buonconsiglio, Caprioli, Benedetto Carpaccio, Fogolino, Giorgionesque Paintings, Licinio, Montagnana, Niccolò di Pietro, Palma Vecchio, Pasqualino di Niccolò, Previtali, Quirizio da Murano, Francesco da Santacroce, Girolamo da Santacroce.

S. FRANCESCO: Cariani.

BEATA VERGINE DEL SOCCORSO (LA ROTONDA): Filippo da Verona.

Roxley House (Letchworth, Herts.). MR. H. BENDIXSON (EX): Lotto.

Rutigliano (Bari). S. MARIA DELLA COLONNA: Antonio Vivarini.

Sacramento (Florida). E. B. CROCKER ART GALLERY: Bonifazio Veronese.

Saint Albans (Herts.). BEECHWOOD PARK, SIR GILES SEBRIGHT (EX): Sebastiano del Piombo.

Saint-Germain-en-Laye. MUSÉE DE LA VILLE: Andrea Schiavone.

Saint-Lô. MUSÉE: Jacobello del Fiore.

Saint Louis (Missouri). CITY ART MUSEUM: Francesco de' Franceschi, Paolo Veronese, Tintoretto, Titian.

WASHINGTON UNIVERSITY: Lotto.

MR. EDWARD A. FAUST: Tintoretto.

Saletto (Este). CHIESA PARROCCHIALE: Licinio.

Salò (Lago di Garda). DUOMO: Paolo Veneziano.

Saltwood Castle (Kent). SIR KENNETH CLARK: Giovanni Bellini, Tintoretto.

San Benedetto Po (Mantua). ABRAZIA DI POLIRONE: Bordone.

San Daniele del Friuli (Udine). SAN MICHELE (DUOMO): Amalteo, Pordenone.

S. ANTONIO: Giambono, Pellegrino da San Daniele.

San Diego (California). FINE ARTS GALLERY: Giovanni Bellini, Jacopo Bellini, Cariani, Carlo Crivelli, Licinio, Lorenzo Veneziano, Palma Vecchio, Paolo Veronese, Girolamo da Santacroce, Francesco Vecellio.

PUTNAM FOUNDATION: Paolo Veronese, Titian.

San Fior di Sopra (Treviso). CHIESA PARROCCHIALE: Cima.

San Floriano in Campagna (Treviso). CHIESA PARROCCHIALE: Bissolo.

San Francisco (California). M. H. DE YOUNG MEMORIAL MUSEUM: Gentile Bellini, Bonifazio Veronese, Bartolomeo Montagna, Palma Vecchio, Polidoro, Pordenone, Tintoretto, Titian, Bartolomeo Vivarini.

CALIFORNIA PALACE OF THE LEGION OF HONOR: Lotto, Paolo Veronese, Tintoretto.

Sangallo (Bergamo). S. MARIA ASSUNTA: Boldrini.

San Ginesio (Macerata). MUNICIPIO: Folchetti.

COLLEGIATA: Alamanno, Folchetti.

S. GREGORIO: Folchetti.

S. MICHELE: Folchetti.

San Giorgio in Velo d'Astico (Vicenza). S. GIORGIO: Speranza.

San Giovanni di Biagio (Como). GIBERT COLLECTION: Giambono.

San Giovanni Ilarione (Vicenza). CHIESA DEL CASTELLO: Bartolomeo Montagna.

San Luca di Crosara (Vicenza). CHIESA PARROCCHIALE: Jacopo Bassano.

San Marino. MUNICIPIO: Giambono.

San Marino (California). HUNTINGTON MUSEUM: Giovanni Bellini.

San Martino al Tagliamento (Udine). S. MARTINO: Amalteo.

San Martino dei Calvi (Bergamo). S. MARTINO: Lattanzio da Rimini.

San Niccolò del Comelico (Belluno). CHIESA PARROCCHIALE: Gianfrancesco da Tolmezzo.

San Pietro d'Orzio (Bergamo). S. PIETRO A SAN GIOVANNI BIANCO: Venetian fifteenth-century unidentified.

San Severino (Macerata). PINACOTECA CIVICA: Vittorio Crivelli, Paolo Veneziano.

San Simone di Vallada (Belluno). CHIESA PARROCCHIALE: Bordone.

San Vendemiano (Treviso). CHIESA PARROCCHIALE: Silvio.

San Vito al Tagliamento (Udine). S. MARIA DEI BATTUTI: Amalteo.

DUOMO: Amalteo, Bellunello.

S. LORENZO: Bellunello.

San Vito di Cadore (Belluno). BEATA VERGINE DELLA DIFESA: Francesco Vecellio.

CHIESA PIEVANALE: Francesco Vecellio.

Sankt Florian (Linz). GEMÄLDESAMMLUNG: Jacopo Bassano, Leandro Bassano, Polidoro, Andrea Schiavone.

Sant'Agata Feltria (Urbino). CONGREGAZIONE DI CARITÀ: Nicola di Maestro Antonio d'Ancona.

Sant'Arcangelo di Romagna (Forlì). MUNICIPIO: Jacobello di Bonomo.

Santa Barbara (California). MRS. C. FELTON (EX): Pasqualino di Niccolò.

Santa Caterina di Lusiana (Vicenza). CHIESA PARROCCHIALE: Jacopo Bassano.

Santa Cristina al Tivarone (Treviso). CHIESA PARROCCHIALE: Lotto.

Sant' Elpidio Morico (Ascoli Piceno). S. ELPIDIO: Vittorio Crivelli.

Sant' Elpidio a Mare (Ascoli Piceno). PALAZZO COMUNALE: Vittorio Crivelli.

Santa Monica (California). J. PAUL GETTY MUSEUM: Bartolomeo Veneto, Giovanni Bellini, Bonifazio Veronese, Cariani, Lotto, Paolo Veronese, Tintoretto, Titian.

São Paulo (Brazil). MUSEUM: Giovanni Bellini, Antonio Rosso da Cadore, Titian.

Sarasota (Florida). JOHN AND MABLE RINGLING MUSEUM: Gentile Bellini, Follower of Giovanni Bellini, Bonifazio Veronese, Buscatti, Lotto, Mazzola, Palma Vecchio, Paolo Veneziano, Paolo Veronese, Pordenone, Sebastiano del Piombo, Tintoretto.

Sarcedo (Vicenza). CHIESA PARROCCHIALE: Verla.

Sargnano (Belluno). CHIESA PARROCCHIALE: Cesa.

Sarmego (Vicenza). CHIESA PARROCCHIALE: Bartolomeo Montagna.

Sarnano (Macerata). MUNICIPIO: Alamanno, Folchetti.

    S. FRANCESCO: Vittorio Crivelli.

Sassari. PINACOTECA: Bartolomeo Vivarini.

    DUOMO: Close to Antonello da Messina.

Sassoferrato (Ancona). MUSEO CIVICO: Agapiti.

    S. CROCE: Agapiti.

    S. FORTUNATO: Agapiti.

    S. MARIA DEL PIANO: Agapiti.

    S. PIETRO: Agapiti.

Schio (Vicenza). S. FRANCESCO: Dario da Treviso, Speranza, Verla.

Schleissheim. GEMÄLDEGALERIE: Sustris.

Schwerin. MECKLENBURGISCHES LANDESMUSEUM: Leandro Bassano, Bartolomeo Montagna, Tintoretto.

Seattle (Washington). ART MUSEUM: Paolo Veronese, Previtali, Tintoretto, Bartolomeo Vivarini.

Sebenico see **Sibenik.**

Sedgehill Grange (Shaftesbury, Dorset). MR. NIEL RIMINGTON: Marconi.

Sedico (Belluno). CHIESA ARCIPRETALE: Mariscalchi, Francesco Vecellio.

Sedrina (Bergamo). S. GIACOMO: Lotto, Silvio.

Selva di Cadore (Belluno). S. LORENZO: Giovanni da Mel, Montagnana, Antonio Rosso da Cadore.

Senigallia (Ancona). CONTI AUGUSTI ARSILLI: Sebastiano del Piombo.

Seriate (Bergamo). PICCINELLI COLLECTION (EX): Cariani.

Serina (Bergamo). SS. ANNUNZIATA: Palma Vecchio, Previtali, Francesco da Santacroce.

Shenfield Mill (Theale, Berks.). DR. J. HASSON: Tintoretto.

Sibenik (Dalmatia). CONVENTO DI S. LORENZO: Andrea da Murano.

Sibiu (Roumania). BRUCKENTHAL GALLERY: Antonello da Messina, Lotto.

Siena. PINACOTECA: Bordone, Lotto.

Sinaia (Roumania). CASTLE OF PELISOR: Antonello de Saliba, Lotto.

Socchieve (Udine). S. MARTINO: Gianfrancesco da Tolmezzo.

Solagna (Vicenza). CHIESA PARROCCHIALE: Francesco Bassano.

Sossano (Vicenza). CHIESA PARROCCHIALE: Jacopo Bassano (depos. at Bassano del Grappa).

Southampton (New York). PARRISH ART MUSEUM: Buonconsiglio, Fogolino, Lotto, Mazzola.

South Bend (Indiana). UNIVERSITY OF NOTRE DAME: Bartolomeo Veneto.

Spalato see **Split.**

Spilimbergo (Udine). DUOMO: Giovanni Martini da Udine, Pordenone

Spinea (Venice). CHIESA PARROCCHIALE: Belliniano.

Split (Dalmatia). DUOMO: Giovanni and Bernardino da Asola.

GALLERIA BANOVINSKA: Andrea Schiavone.

S. MARIA DELLE GRAZIE ALLE PALUDI: Lotto, Girolamo da Santacroce.

Spoleto. GALLERIA CIVICA: Antonello de Saliba.

Springfield (Mass.). ART MUSEUM: Jacopo Bassano, Bartolomeo Montagna.

Stezzano (Bergamo). SANTUARIO DELLA MADONNA DEI CAMPI: Previtali.

Stockholm. NATIONAL MUSEUM: Giovanni Bellini, Bonifazio Veronese, Carrari da Forlì, Jacobello del Fiore, Lotto, Paolo Veronese, Girolamo da Santacroce, Andrea Schiavone, Tintoretto.

UNIVERSITY GALLERY: Sustris.

HERR KARL LUNDMARK: Girolamo dei Maggi.

HERR R. PETRE: Diana.

DR. C. SANDSTRÖM: Sebastiano del Piombo.

Stourhead (Wilts.). NATIONAL TRUST: Leandro Bassano.

Strasbourg. MUSÉE DES BEAUX-ARTS: Basaiti, Jacopo Bassano, Bordone, Cariani, Cima, Carlo Crivelli, Marconi, Mazzola, Bartolomeo Montagna, Palma Vecchio, Paolo Veronese, Pellegrino da San Daniele, Quirizio da Murano, Speranza, Tintoretto.

Stuttgart. GEMÄLDEGALERIE: Leandro Bassano, Bastiani, Giovanni Bellini, Bello, Bonifazio Veronese, Bordone, Vittore Carpaccio, Diana, Giovanni di Francia, Jacobello del Fiore, Mansueti, Marconi, Palma Vecchio, Paolo Veronese, Rondinelli, Tintoretto, Titian, Venetian sixteenth-century unidentified.

KING OF WÜRTTEMBERG (EX): Tintoretto.

Susegana (Treviso). CHIESA PARROCCHIALE: Pordenone.

Sutton Place (Surrey). DUKE OF SUTHERLAND: Tintoretto.

Syon House (Isleworth, Middx.). DUKE OF NORTHUMBERLAND: Paolo Veronese. (See also **Albury Park** and **Alnwick Castle.**)

Syracuse. MUSEO NAZIONALE DI PALAZZO BELLOMO: Antonello da Messina, Lorenzo Veneziano, Solario.

DUOMO: Antonello de Saliba.

PALAZZO ARCIVESCOVILE: Antonello de Saliba.

Taibon (Belluno). CHIESA PARROCCHIALE: Bordone.

Taormina (Messina). DUOMO: Antonello de Saliba.

Taranto. MUSEO: Bartolomeo Vivarini.

Tarrytown-on-Hudson (New York). MR. J. J. CHAPMAN (EX): Follower of Gentile Bellini.

Teramo (Abruzzi). MUNICIPIO: Jacobello del Fiore.

Terlago (Trent). S. PANTALEONE: Verla.

Terlizzi (Bari). CHIESA DEGLI OSSERVANTI: Pordenone, Savoldo.

Terzo (Udine). S. GIOVANNI: Domenico di Candido da Tolmezzo.

Terzo d'Aquileia (Udine). CALLIGARIS COLLECTION: Florigerio.

Thiene (Vicenza). CASTELLO COLLEONI: Girolamo da Vicenza, Zelotti.

Tiflis (U.S.S.R.). GALLERY: Paolo Veneziano.

Toledo. CATEDRAL: Leandro Bassano, Giovanni Bellini.

Toledo (Ohio). MUSEUM OF ART: Bastiani, Giovanni Bellini, Bissolo.

Tolmezzo (Udine). S. CATERINA: Amalteo.

Torcello see **Venice** (Environs).

Toronto (Canada). ART GALLERY: Bordone.

Torre di Palme (Fermo). S. GIOVANNI BATTISTA: Vittorio Crivelli.

S. MARIA A MARE: Jacobello di Bonomo.

Torre di Pordenone (Udine). CHIESA PARROCCHIALE: Pordenone.

Torre San Patrizio (Fermo). MADONNA DELLA ROSA: Alamanno.

Tours. MUSÉE DES BEAUX-ARTS: Jacopo Bassano, Bissolo.

Trani (Bari). DUOMO: Giovanni di Francia.

Traù (Dalmatia). CATTEDRALE: Gentile Bellini.

Travesio (Udine). S. PIETRO: Pordenone.

Trebasèleghe (Padua). CHIESA PARROCCHIALE: Andrea da Murano.

Trent. CASTELLO DEL BUONCONSIGLIO: Fogolino.

   MUSEO NAZIONALE DEL TRENTINO: Fogolino.

   S. VIGILIO (DUOMO): Verla.

   PALAZZO SARDAGNA: Fogolino.

   PIAZZA DEL DUOMO. CASA RELLA: Fogolino.

Trescore (Bergamo). ORATORIO SUARDI: Lotto.

Tresto (Este). CHIESA DELLA MADONNA: Bissolo, Montagnana.

Treviso. MUSEO CIVICO (PINACOTECA): Antonio Maria da Carpi, Jacopo Bassano Becca-
   ruzzi, Giovanni Bellini, Bordone, Caprioli, Cima, Francesco da Milano, Girolamo da
   Treviso, Lotto, Pellegrino da San Daniele, Pordenone, Antonio Rosso da Cadore,
   Girolamo da Santacroce, Titian, Vincenzo dalle Destre.

   S. ANDREA: Bissolo.

   S. LEONARDO: Cima, Vincenzo dalle Destre.

   S. NICCOLÒ: Andrea da Murano, Lotto, Savoldo, Venetian sixteenth-century unidentified.

   S. PIETRO (DUOMO): Amalteo, Bissolo, Bordone, Caprioli, Girolamo da Treviso, Pordenone, Titian.

   MONTE DI PIETÀ: Beccaruzzi, Girolamo da Treviso (ex), Venetian sixteenth-century unidentified.

   CONVENTO DI S. PARISIO (EX): Beccaruzzi.

   CONTE AGOSTI: Mariscalchi.

Trieste. MUSEO DI STORIA E D'ARTE: Jacobello del Fiore, Bartolomeo Montagna, Paolo
   Veneziano, Pasqualino di Niccolò, Pellegrino da San Daniele, Veneto-Byzantine Painter.

   S. GIUSTO: Benedetto Carpaccio.

   FRANCESCO BASILIO COLLECTION (EX): Francesco da Santacroce.

Tucson. UNIVERSITY OF ARIZONA: Cariani, Vittorio Crivelli, Florigerio.

Tulsa (Oklahoma). PHILBROOK ART CENTER: Giovanni Bellini, Cariani, Vittore Carpaccio,
   Andrea Schiavone.

Tunis. VICTOR GUEZ COLLECTION: Lotto.

Turin. GALLERIA SABAUDA: Antonello da Messina, Close to Antonello da Messina, Giovanni
   Bellini, Follower of Giovanni Bellini, Cariani, Diana, Mazzola, Bartolomeo Montagna,
   Nicola di Maestro Antonio d'Ancona, Palma Vecchio, Paolo da Brescia, Paolo
   Veneziano, Paolo Veronese, Girolamo da Santacroce, Savoldo, Andrea Schiavone,
   Tintoretto, Bartolomeo Vivarini.

   ACCADEMIA ALBERTINA: Filippo da Verona, Jacopo da Valenza, Polidoro.

   MUSEO CIVICO DI PALAZZO MADAMA: Antonello da Messina, Antonio Vivarini.

Turriaco (Trieste). S. ROCCO: Grassi.

Ubeda (Andalusia). S. SALVADOR: Sebastiano del Piombo.

Udine. MUSEO CIVICO: Amalteo, Niccolò de' Barbari, Bellunello, Vittore Carpaccio,
   Domenico di Candido da Tolmezzo, Giorgionesque Paintings, Girolamo da Udine,
   Giovanni Martini da Udine, Pellegrino da San Daniele, Pordenone.

MUNICIPIO: Amalteo.

ANNUNZIATA (DUOMO): Amalteo, Grassi, Giovanni Martini da Udine, Pellegrino da San Daniele, Pordenone.

S. GIORGIO: Florigerio.

MADONNA DELLE GRAZIE: Monverde.

S. PIETRO MARTIRE: Amalteo, Giovanni Martini da Udine.

OSPEDALE DEI PELLEGRINI: Grassi.

CONTE CERNAZAI (EX): Girolamo da Santacroce.

FLORIO COLLECTION: Giovanni Martini da Udine.

Umtali (Southern Rhodesia). MAJOR STEPHEN COURTAULD: Paolo Veronese.

Upton House (Banbury, Oxon.). NATIONAL TRUST: Carlo Crivelli, Lotto, Sustris, Tintoretto.

Urbino. GALLERIA NAZIONALE DI PALAZZO DUCALE: Alamanno, Basaiti, Carlo Crivelli, Mansueti, Nicola di Maestro Antonio d'Ancona, Rondinelli, Titian, Alvise Vivarini.

Urbisaglia (Macerata). COLLEGIATA: Folchetti.

(Environs). CHIESETTA DELLA MAESTÀ: Folchetti.

S. MARIA DI BRUSCIANO: Folchetti.

Vacile (Lestans, Udine). S. LORENZO: Pordenone.

Vaduz. FÜRSTLICH LIECHTENSTEINSCHE SAMMLUNG: Basaiti, Giovanni Bellini, Bordone, Catena, Vittorio Crivelli, Lattanzio da Rimini, Licinio, Mansueti, Mazzola, Palma Vecchio, Francesco Vecellio.

Valdobbiàdene (Treviso). CHIESA ARCIPRETALE: Beccaruzzi, Bordone.

Valeriano (Udine). S. MARIA DEI BATTUTI: Pordenone.

S. STEFANO: Pordenone.

Valle di Cadore (Belluno). S. MARTINO: Francesco da Milano.

Vallenoncello (Udine). CHIESA PARROCCHIALE: Pordenone.

Vallesella (Belluno). CHIESA ARCIPRETALE: Francesco Vecellio.

Valstagna (Vicenza). CHIESA PARROCCHIALE: Francesco Bassano.

Valvasone (Udine). CHIESA PARROCCHIALE: Amalteo.

Varmo (Udine). S. LORENZO: Pordenone.

Velletri (Rome). MUSEO CAPITOLARE: Giovanni di Francia.

Velo d'Astico (Vicenza). CHIESA PARROCCHIALE: Verla.

Venas (Belluno). CHIESA PARROCCHIALE: Francesco Vecellio.

Venice. ACCADEMIA: Andrea da Murano, Antonello de Saliba, Basaiti, Jacopo Bassano, Leandro Bassano, Bastiani, Beccaruzzi, Gentile Bellini, Giovanni Bellini, Follower of Giovanni Bellini, Jacopo Bellini, Bello, Bissolo, Bonifazio Veronese, Bordone, Buonconsiglio, Busati, Buscatti, Campagnola, Cariani, Vittore Carpaccio, Caterino Veneziano, Catena, Cima, Carlo Crivelli, Diana, Florigerio, Fogolino, Francesco de' Franceschi, Francesco da Milano, Giambono, Gianfrancesco da Tolmezzo, Giorgione, Giorgione Copies, Giovanni da Bologna, Girolamo da Treviso, Ingannati, Jacobello del Fiore, Jacopo da Valenza, Licinio, Lorenzo Veneziano, Lotto, Mansueti, Marconi, Marziale, Bartolomeo Montagna, Montagnana, Montemezzano, Niccolò di Pietro, Palma Vecchio, Paolo Veneziano, Paolo Veronese, Pennacchi, Polidoro, Pordenone, Previtali, Quirizio da Murano, Rondinelli, Antonio Rosso da Cadore, Francesco da Santacroce, Girolamo da Santacroce, Savoldo, Andrea Schiavone, Simone da Cusighe, Stefano di Sant'Agnese, Sustris, Tintoretto, Titian, Francesco Vecellio, Alvise Vivarini, Antonio Vivarini, Bartolomeo Vivarini, Zelotti, Venetian fifteenth-century unidentified.

GALLERIA FRANCHETTI ALLA CA'D'ORO: Bartolomeo Veneto, Giovanni Bellini, Follower of Giovanni Bellini, Bordone, Busati, Vittore Carpaccio, Cima, Diana, Domenico di Candido da Tolmezzo, Duia, Filippo da Verona, Francesco de' Franceschi, Giambono, Licinio, Lorenzo Veneziano, Pordenone, Tintoretto, Alvise Vivarini, Antonio Vivarini, Bartolomeo Vivarini.

LIBRERIA SANSOVINIANA: Paolo Veronese, Andrea Schiavone, Tintoretto, Titian, Zelotti.

MUSEO STORICO DELL' ARSENALE: Sustris.

MUSEO CIVICO CORRER: Antonello da Messina, Basaiti, Leandro Bassano, Bastiani, Gentile Bellini, Follower of Gentile Bellini, Giovanni Bellini, Jacopo Bellini, Bissolo, Boldrini, Vittore Carpaccio, Catena, Cima, Duia, Filippo da Verona, Francesco de' Franceschi, Giambono, Giovanni da Bologna, Giovanni and Bernardino da Asola, Giovanni di Francia, Ingannati, Jacobello del Fiore, Jacopo da Valenza, Lorenzo Veneziano, Lotto, Mansueti, Giovanni Martini da Udine, Marziale, Mazzola, Mocetto, Bartolomeo Montagna, Paolo Veneziano, Pasqualino di Niccolò, Rondinelli, Francesco da Santacroce, Girolamo da Santacroce, Stefano di Sant'Agnese, Tintoretto, Vincenzo dalle Destre, Alvise Vivarini, Bartolomeo Vivarini, Veneto-Byzantine Painters, Venetian fifteenth-century unidentified.

MUSEO DI S. MARCO: Gentile Bellini.

PALAZZO DUCALE: Antonello de Saliba, Jacopo Bassano, Leandro Bassano, Giovanni Bellini, Bonifazio Veronese, Bordone, Bragadin, Vittore Carpaccio, Jacobello del Fiore, Paolo Veronese, Sustris, Tintoretto, Titian, Zelotti.

PALAZZO REALE (EX): Girolamo da Santacroce.

PALAZZO DONÀ DELLE ROSE (EX): Bartolomeo Veneto, Leandro Bassano.

PINACOTECA QUERINI STAMPALIA: Jacopo Bassano, Giovanni Bellini, Bonifazio Veronese, Bordone, Caterino Veneziano, Catena, Duia, Giorgione Copies, Giovanni and Bernardino da Asola, Palma Vecchio, Francesco da Santacroce, Girolamo da Santacroce, Andrea Schiavone.

SEMINARIO PATRIARCALE, PINACOTECA MANFREDINIANA: Follower of Gentile Bellini, Caselli da Parma, Cima, Giorgione, Giovanni di Francia, Paolo Veronese, Alvise Vivarini, Antonio Vivarini.

ISOLA DI S. GIORGIO MAGGIORE. GIORGIO CINI FOUNDATION: Bonifazio Veronese, Paolo Veronese, Sustris, Tintoretto.

S. ALVISE: Jacobello del Fiore.

S. ALVISE, INSTITUTO DELLE SUORE CANOSSIANE: Paolo Veneziano.

S. ANDREA DELLA ZIRADA: Bordone, Paolo Veronese.

ANGELO RAFFAELE: Bonifazio Veronese.

S. ANTONINO: Bastiani.

SS. APOSTOLI: Veneto-Byzantine Painter.

S. BARNABA: Giovanni and Bernardino da Asola, Paolo Veronese.

S. BARTOLOMEO IN RIALTO: Sebastiano del Piombo.

S. CASSIANO: Leandro Bassano, Palma Vecchio, Tintoretto.

S. CATERINA: Tintoretto.

S. CRISOGONO: Rondinelli.

S. EUFEMIA: Bartolomeo Vivarini.

S. FANTINO: Duia.

S. FELICE: Tintoretto.

S. FRANCESCO DELLA VIGNA: Antonio da Negroponte, Giovanni Bellini, Diana, Giorgione

Copies, Montemezzano, Oliverio, Paolo Veronese, Girolamo da Santacroce, Antonio Vivarini, Zelotti.

S. GIACOMO DELL'ORIO: Jacopo Bassano, Buonconsiglio, Lotto, Paolo Veronese, Andrea Schiavone.

S. GIOBBE: Bordone, Previtali, Savoldo, Antonio Vivarini.

S. GIORGIO DEGLI SCHIAVONI: Benedetto Carpaccio, Vittore Carpaccio.

S. GIORGIO MAGGIORE: Jacopo Bassano, Leandro Bassano, Vittore Carpaccio, Tintoretto.

S. GIOVANNI IN BRAGORA: Bissolo, Bordone, Cima, Jacobello del Fiore, Alvise Vivarini, Bartolomeo Vivarini.

S. GIOVANNI DEI CAVALIERI: Giovanni Bellini.

S. GIOVANNI CRISOSTOMO: Giovanni Bellini, Giorgione, Girolamo da Santacroce, Sebastiano del Piombo.

S. GIOVANNI ELEMOSINARIO: Pordenone, Titian.

SS. GIOVANNI E PAOLO: Leandro Bassano, Giovanni Bellini, Bonifazio Veronese, Cima, Lotto, Marconi, Mocetto, Paolo Veronese, Bartolomeo Vivarini.

S. GIULIANO: Leandro Bassano, Paolo Veronese, Girolamo da Santacroce.

S. GIUSEPPE DI CASTELLO: Paolo Veronese, Tintoretto.

S. LIO: Titian.

S. LAZZARO DEI MENDICANTI: Paolo Veronese, Tintoretto.

S. LUCA: Paolo Veronese.

S. MARCO: Leandro Bassano, Bastiani, Gentile Bellini, Giambono, Paolo Veneziano, Pordenone, Tintoretto, Antonio Vivarini, Bartolomeo Vivarini.

S. MARCUOLA: Tintoretto, Titian.

MADONNA DELL'ORTO: Beccaruzzi, Giovanni Bellini, Cima, Tintoretto.

S. MARIA ASSUNTA (GESUITI): Tintoretto, Titian.

S. MARIA DEL CARMELO (I CARMINI): Cima, Lotto, Andrea Schiavone, Venetian sixteenth-century unidentified.

S. MARIA FORMOSA: Leandro Bassano, Palma Vecchio, Pietro da Messina, Bartolomeo Vivarini.

S. MARIA DEI FRARI: Basaiti, Giovanni Bellini, Licinio, Paolo Veneziano, Titian, Alvise Vivarini, Bartolomeo Vivarini.

S. MARIA MATER DOMINI: Bissolo, Catena, Tintoretto.

S. MARIA DEI MIRACOLI: Caprioli, Niccolò di Pietro, Pennacchi.

S. MARIA DEL ROSARIO (GESUATI): Tintoretto.

S. MARIA DELLA SALUTE: Basaiti, Giovanni Bellini, Jacopo da Valenza, Oliverio, Polidoro, Tintoretto, Titian.

S. MARIA DELLA VISITAZIONE: Agapiti.

S. MARIA DELLE ZITELLE: Leandro Bassano.

S. MARIA ZOBENIGO: Tintoretto.

S. MARTINO: Girolamo da Santacroce.

S. MARZIALE: Tintoretto, Titian.

S. MOISÈ: Tintoretto.

S. NICCOLÒ DEI MENDICOLI: Montemezzano.

S. PANTALEONE: Paolo Veronese, Antonio Vivarini.

S. PIETRO DI CASTELLO: Basaiti, Paolo Veronese.

S. POLO: Paolo Veronese, Tintoretto.

REDENTORE: Andrea da Murano, Bissolo, Marconi, Paolo Veronese, Pennacchi, Alvise Vivarini.

S. ROCCO: Pordenone, Tintoretto.

S. SALVATORE: Giovanni Bellini, Titian, Francesco Vecellio.

S. SAMUELE: Paolo Veneziano.

SCALZI (S. MARIA DI NAZARETH): Giovanni Bellini.

S. SEBASTIANO: Bonifazio Veronese, Paolo Veronese, Girolamo da Santacroce, Andrea Schiavone, Titian.

S. SILVESTRO: Girolamo da Santacroce, Tintoretto.

S. SIMEONE GRANDE: Mansueti, Tintoretto.

S. SPIRITO: Buonconsiglio.

S. STEFANO: Bonifazio Veronese, Pordenone, Tintoretto, Antonio Vivarini.

S. TROVASO: Catena, Giambono, Jacobello del Fiore, Tintoretto.

S. VITALE: Vittore Carpaccio.

S. ZACCARIA: Leandro Bassano, Giovanni Bellini, Diana, Francesco da Santacroce, Stefano di Sant'Agnese, Tintoretto, Antonio Vivarini.

SCUOLA GRANDE DI S. MARCO: Belliniano, Bordone, Mansueti, Palma Vecchio, Girolamo da Santacroce, Tintoretto.

SCUOLA GRANDE DI S. ROCCO: Giorgione, Tintoretto, Titian.

ENRICO ALBUZIO (EX): Giorgione Copies.

ITALICO BRASS COLLECTION: Leandro Bassano, Mansueti, Pordenone, Andrea Schiavone, Sustris, Titian, Bartolomeo Vivarini.

CONTE VITTORIO CINI: Jacopo de' Barbari, Bartolomeo Veneto, Giovanni Bellini, Bonifazio Veronese, Bordone, Caprioli, Cariani, Cima, Carlo Crivelli, Diana, Francesco de Bais Imolese, Giorgione, Licinio, Lorenzo Veneziano, Lotto, Mansueti, Bartolomeo Montagna, Paolo Veronese, Pietro da Messina, Andrea Schiavone, Sebastiano del Piombo, Stefano di Sant'Agnese, Tintoretto, Bartolomeo Vivarini, Venetian fifteenth-century unidentified.

SIG. A. COIN: Andrea Schiavone.

FORTI COLLECTION: Close to Antonello da Messina.

GIOVANNELLI COLLECTION (EX): Caprioli, Lotto, Marconi, Palma Vecchio.

GIUSTINIANI COLLECTION (EX): Girolamo da Treviso, Pasqualino di Niccolò.

GUGGENHEIM COLLECTION (EX): Fogolino.

SALVADORI COLLECTION (EX): Lattanzio da Rimini.

PROF. TULLIO SPANIO: Giorgione Copies.

CONTE PINO DI VALMARANA (EX): Paolo Veronese.

DALLA ZONCA COLLECTION (EX): Mancini.

Venice (Environs). BURANO, S. MARTINO: Mansueti, Girolamo da Santacroce.

— MURANO, MUSEO VETRARIO: Andrea da Murano, Bastiani, Diana, Paolo Veronese, Polidoro, Quirizio da Murano, Bartolomeo Vivarini.

— — SS. MARIA E DONATO: Bastiani.

— — S. MARIA DEGLI ANGELI: Pordenone, Rondinelli.

— — S. PIETRO MARTIRE: Giovanni Bellini, Paolo Veronese, Rondinelli, Francesco da Santacroce.

— TORCELLO, MUSEO PROVINCIALE: Paolo Veronese.

— — ASSUNTA (CATTEDRALE): Tintoretto, Zannino di Pietro.

— — S. FOSCA: Bonifazio Veronese.

Venzone (Udine). PALAZZO COMUNALE: Amalteo.

Verbosca (Island of Hvar, Dalmatia). S. LORENZO: Jacopo Bassano, Paolo Veronese.

Vercelli. MUSEO BORGOGNA: Bissolo, Ingannati, Licinio, Palma Vecchio, Girolamo da Santacroce, Titian.

Verona. MUSEO CIVICO DI CASTELVECCHIO: Antonello da Messina, Antonello de Saliba, Jacopo de' Barbari, Basaiti, Jacopo Bassano, Leandro Bassano, Bastiani, Giovanni Bellini, Jacopo Bellini, Bissolo, Vittore Carpaccio, Cima, Carlo Crivelli, Diana, Fogolino, Francesco de' Franceschi, Giambono, Gianfrancesco da Tolmezzo, Giorgione Copies, Ingannati, Jacopo da Valenza, Mansueti, Mariscalchi, Giovanni Martini da Udine, Marziale, Mocetto, Bartolomeo Montagna, Paolo Veronese, Previtali, Francesco da Santacroce, Girolamo da Santacroce, Tintoretto, Titian, Francesco Vecellio, Verla, Alvise Vivarini, Antonio Vivarini, Zelotti.

PALAZZO DELLA GRAN GUARDIA: Paolo Veronese.

DUOMO: Titian.

S. FIDENZIO (EX): Verla.

S. GIORGIO IN BRAIDA: Montemezzano, Paolo Veronese.

S. MARIA IN ORGANO: Mocetto, Savoldo.

SS. NAZZARO E CELSO: Mocetto, Bartolomeo Montagna.

S. PAOLO: Paolo Veronese.

S. TOSCANA: Domenico di Candido da Tolmezzo.

CONTE J. GIUSTI DEL GIARDINO: Jacopo Bassano.

CONTE SALVI PINDEMONTE MOSCARDO (EX): Paolo Veronese.

Vertova (Bergamo). S. MARIA ASSUNTA: Galizzi.

Verucchio (Forlì). PALAZZO COMUNALE: Niccolò di Pietro.

Viadana (Mantua). S. MARTINO: Leandro Bassano.

Vicenza. MUSEO CIVICO: Antonello de Saliba, Jacopo Bassano, Leandro Bassano, Follower of Giovanni Bellini, Buonconsiglio, Busati, Cariani, Cima, Diana, Fogolino, Licinio, Lotto, Mansueti, Mocetto, Bartolomeo Montagna, Benedetto Montagna, Paolo Veneziano, Paolo Veronese, Francesco da Santacroce, Girolamo da Santacroce, Antonio Solario, Speranza, Sustris, Tintoretto, Francesco Vecellio, Zelotti.

DUOMO: Buonconsiglio, Lorenzo Veneziano, Bartolomeo Montagna.

S. CORONA: Leandro Bassano, Giovanni Bellini, Fogolino, Bartolomeo Montagna, Paolo Veronese, Speranza.

S. DOMENICO: Fogolino, Speranza.

S. LORENZO: Bartolomeo Montagna.

S. MARIA DEL CARMINE: Benedetto Montagna.

S. MARIA DELLE GRAZIE: Leandro Bassano.

S. MARIA DEI SERVI: Benedetto Montagna.

S. PIETRO: Zelotti.

S. ROCCO: Zelotti.

S. STEFANO: Palma Vecchio.

VESCOVADO: Zelotti.

(Environs). BASILICA DI MONTE BERICO: Bartolomeo Montagna, Paolo Veronese.

Vienna. KUNSTHISTORISCHES MUSEUM: Antonello da Messina, Jacopo de' Barbari, Basaiti, Jacopo Bassano, Leandro Bassano, Gentile Bellini, Giovanni Bellini, Bonifazio Veronese, Bordone, Cariani, Catena, Giorgione, Giorgione Copies, Girolamo di Tommaso da Treviso, Licinio, Lotto, Mancini, Montemezzano, Palma Vecchio, Paolo Veronese, Polidoro, Pordenone, Previtali, Savoldo, Andrea Schiavone, Sebastiano del Piombo, Sustris, Tintoretto, Titian, Francesco Vecellio, Alvise Vivarini, Antonio Vivarini, Venetian fifteenth-century unidentified.

AKADEMIE: Filippo da Verona, Ingannati, Pellegrino da San Daniele, Polidoro, Girolamo da Santacroce, Andrea Schiavone, Titian.

LIECHTENSTEIN GALERIE (EX): Follower of Gentile Bellini, Tintoretto.

VON AUSPITZ COLLECTION (EX): Jacopo Bassano, Mansueti, Pellegrino da San Daniele, Pordenone, Girolamo da Santacroce.

RITTER VON BRUDERMANN COLLECTION (EX): Gentile Bellini.

CZERNIN COLLECTION: Bordone, Marconi.

DR. HERMANN EISLER (EX): Vittore Carpaccio, Carlo Crivelli, Pordenone.

DR. HUGO HABEFELD (EX): Ingannati.

HARRACH COLLECTION (EX): Licinio.

GRAF LANCKORONSKI: Bonifazio Veronese, Buonconsiglio (ex), Vittorio Crivelli, Jacobello del Fiore (ex), Bartolomeo Montagna.

LEDERER COLLECTION (EX): Jacopo Bellini, Girolamo da Treviso, Jacobello del Fiore, Polidoro.

MIELTKE COLLECTION (EX): Cariani.

MOLL COLLECTION (EX): Tintoretto.

OFENHEIM COLLECTION (EX): Lotto, Tintoretto.

PANTHER COLLECTION (EX): Sustris.

BARON LOUIS DE ROTHSCHILD (EX): Tintoretto.

BARON TUCHER (EX): Sebastiano del Piombo.

WITTGENSTEIN COLLECTION (EX): Giovanni Bellini.

Vierhouten (Otterlo). VAN BEUNINGEN COLLECTION: Follower of Gentile Bellini, Paolo Veronese, Polidoro, Tintoretto, Titian.

Vigonza (Padua). CASA PARROCCHIALE: Montagnana.

Villa di Anzano see **Anzano.**

Villabruna (Feltre). CHIESA PARROCCHIALE: Mariscalchi, Morto da Feltre.

Villanova (San Daniele, Udine). CHIESA PARROCCHIALE: Pordenone.

Viterbo. S. MARIA DELLA VERITÀ (MUSEO CIVICO): Sebastiano del Piombo.

Vittorio Veneto (Treviso). S. MARIA NUOVA (DUOMO DI SERRAVALLE): Francesco da Milano, Titian.

S. MARIA ASSUNTA E S. TIZIANO (CATTEDRALE DI CENEDA): Amalteo, Jacopo da Valenza.

S. ANDREA: Francesco da Milano.

S. GIOVANNI BATTISTA: Francesco da Milano, Jacopo da Valenza.

S. LORENZO (CHIESA DELL'OSPEDALE): Francesco da Milano.

S. MARIA IN MESCHIO: Previtali.

S. SILVESTRO ALLA COSTA: Francesco da Milano.

PALAZZO TROYER: Dario da Treviso.

LOGGIA CENEDESE: Amalteo.

OSPEDALE: Girolamo da Treviso, Venetian fifteenth-century unidentified.

Wantage see **Lockinge House.**

Warsaw. NATIONAL MUSEUM: Giovanni Bellini, Follower of Giovanni Bellini, Bonifazio Veronese, Bordone, Cariani, Cima, Girolamo di Tommaso da Treviso, Ingannati, Morto da Feltre, Tintoretto.

Warwick Castle (Warwicks.). EARL OF WARWICK: Buonconsiglio, Savoldo.

Washington (D.C.): NATIONAL GALLERY OF ART: Antonello da Messina, Bartolomeo Veneto, Basaiti, Jacopo Bassano, Giovanni Bellini, Jacopo Bellini, Bordone, Cariani, Vittore Carpaccio, Catena, Cima. Carlo Crivelli, Giambono, Giorgione, Giorgionesque

Furniture Painters, Ingannati, Lotto, Mazzola, Bartolomeo Montagna, Paolo Veneziano, Paolo Veronese, Savoldo, Sebastiano del Piombo, Tintoretto, Titian, Alvise Vivarini, Antonio Vivarini, Bartolomeo Vivarini.

CORCORAN ART GALLERY: Titian.

D. PHILLIPS MEMORIAL GALLERY: Giorgionesque Furniture Painters.

SMITHSONIAN MUSEUM: Bonifazio Veronese, Rondinelli.

MRS. A. DE LIMUR: Giovanni Bellini.

DUMBARTON OAKS FOUNDATION: Jacobello del Fiore.

Waterford (Conn.). MR. NELSON C. WHITE: Licinio.

Weimar. MUSEUM: Jacopo de'Barbari, Tintoretto.

Welbeck Abbey (Notts.). DUKE OF PORTLAND: Diana.

Welwyn (Herts.). SIR OTTO BEIT (EX): Buonconsiglio, Sustris, Tintoretto.

Westbury (New York). MR. BEEKMAN WINTHROP (EX): Cima.

Westonbirt (Glos.). HOLFORD COLLECTION (EX): Bordone, Diana, Paolo Veronese, Tintoretto. (See also **London.**)

Wiesbaden. STÄDTISCHE KUNSTSAMMLUNG: Bordone.

Wigan. HAIGH HALL see **Balcarres.**

Williamstown (Massachusetts). STERLING AND FRANCINE CLARK ART INSTITUTE: Carlo Crivelli, Mazzola, Bartolomeo Montagna.

Wilton House (Salisbury, Wilts.). EARL OF PEMBROKE AND MONTGOMERY: Lotto, Tintoretto.

Windlestone (Durham). SIR T. C. EDEN (EX): Paolo Veronese.

Windsor Castle. ROYAL COLLECTION: Caprioli, Paolo Veronese.

Winterthur. HERR OSCAR REINHARDT: Jacopo Bassano, Tintoretto.

Woodyates Manor (Salisbury, Wilts.). LADY LUCAS AND DINGWALL: Bartolomeo Montagna.

Worcester (Massachusetts). ART MUSEUM: Follower of Giovanni Bellini, Buonconsiglio (ex), Caterino Veneziano, Carlo Crivelli, Girolamo da Udine, Bartolomeo Montagna, Palma Vecchio, Paolo Veneziano, Rondinelli, Tintoretto, Antonio Vivarini.

MR. PHILIP J. GENTNER (EX): Ingannati, Girolamo da Santacroce.

York. CITY ART GALLERY: Jacopo Bassano, Follower of Giovanni Bellini, Bissolo, Cima, Licinio, Mansueti, Nicola di Maestro Antonio d'Ancona, Palma Vecchio.

Zagreb. MUSEUM: Agapiti, Jacopo Bassano, Giovanni Bellini, Filippo da Verona, Giovanni and Bernardino da Asola, Mazzola, Pasqualino di Niccolò, Polidoro, Francesco Vecellio.

Zara (Dalmatia). S. ANASTASIA (DUOMO): Vittore Carpaccio.

S. FRANCESCO: Bastiani, Giambono.

MONASTERO DI S. MARIA: Giovanni di Francia.

MUSEO DI S. DONATO: Marziale.

Zeil (Württemberg). FÜRST WALDBURG-ZEIL-TRAUCHBURG: Sustris.

Zerman (Treviso). S. ELENA: Palma Vecchio.

Zogno (Bergamo). GRUMELLO DEI ZANCHI, CHIESA PARROCCHIALE: Vittore Carpaccio.

S. LORENZO: Palma Vecchio.

Zuglio Carnico (Udine). S. PIETRO: Domenico di Candido da Tolmezzo.

Zumpano (Cosenza). CHIESA PARROCCHIALE: Bartolomeo Vivarini.

Zurich. ABEGG-STOCKAR COLLECTION: Bastiani, Carlo Crivelli.

DR. HUGELSHOFER (EX): Palma Vecchio.

DR. A. SCHRAFL: Giovanni Bellini, Caselli da Parma, Cima, Oliverio.

Homeless. Agapiti, Agostini, Andrea da Murano, Antonello da Messina, Antonello de Saliba, Antonio Maria da Carpi, Jacopo de'Barbari, Bartolomeo Veneto, Basaiti, Jacopo Bassano, Leandro Bassano, Giovanni Bellini, Follower of Giovanni Bellini, Bonifazio Veronese, Bordone, Cariani, Benedetto Carpaccio, Vittore Carpaccio, Caselli da Parma, Catena, Cima, Filippo da Verona, Folchetti, Francesco de' Franceschi, Gavazzi, Giambono, Giovanni and Bernardino da Asola, Girolamo da Udine, Ingannati, Jacobello di Antonello, Jacobello del Fiore, Lattanzio da Rimini, Lotto, Mansueti, Mariscalchi, Marziale, Mazzola, Mocetto, Bartolomeo Montagna, Montemezzano, Oliverio, Paolo Veronese, Pasqualino di Niccolò, Previtali, Rondinelli, Girolamo da Santacroce, Sebastiano del Piombo, Semitecolo, Antonio Solario, Speranza, Tintoretto, Francesco Vecellio, Verla, Alvise Vivarini, Antonio Vivarini.

ADDENDA ET CORRIGENDA

page 11

Bartolomeo Veneto. *Add:* Budapest. BACK COLLECTION (EX). Portrait of a Man wearing elaborate turban and resting right hand on sphere.
— Florence. UFFIZI. 970. *Add:* (c., dated 1555).

page 12

Bartolomeo Veneto. London. SIR J. C. ROBINSON (EX). *Delete* '(version of Uffizi No. 970)'.

page 15

Jacopo Bassano. Biographical notice. *Read:* ca 1510–1592.

page 16

Jacopo Bassano. Bassano del Grappa, Nos, 8, 9, 10. *Add:* for the Sala dell'Udienza *and for* 'E.' *read:* 1535–36.
— No. 7. *Add:* for the Sala del Consiglio.
— No. 432. *Add:* from the Cloister of S. Francesco.

page 17

Jacopo Bassano. Chicago 39.2239. *Add:* sketch.
— Civezzano. *Should read:* Preaching of the Baptist; in predella, Beheading of the Baptist (with his son Francesco).
Marriage of Catherine; in predella, Martyrdom of Catherine (with his son Francesco).
Meeting at the Golden Gate; in predella, Madonna of Mercy. Sd by Jacopo and his son Francesco.

page 18

Jacopo Bassano. Florence, CONTINI BONACOSSI COLLECTION. Madonna with Infant Baptist and Lamb. *Add:* (u.).
— London. MR. PETER HARRIS. *Add:* variant of Vienna 272.

page 19

Jacopo Bassano. Princeton. *Add:* St. replica of Vienna 272.

page 20

Jacopo Bassano. Sossano. *Add:* from the Chiesa dei Riformati, Asolo. Now transferred to Museo Civico, Bassano del Grappa.

page 48

Paris Bordone. Treviso, DUOMO. *Delete* 'with Donor's *and add:* (portrait of Donor stolen and replaced by copy).

page 57

Vittore Carpaccio. Bergamo 115. *Add:* from the Scuola degli Albanesi.
— Bergamo 162. *Add:* From the dismembered polyptych of S. Fosca.
— Milan, Brera 169, 171. *Add:* From the Scuola degli Albanesi.

page 58

Vittore Carpaccio. Venice, MUSEO CORRER I. 47. *Add:* Ca 1504. From the Scuola degli Albanesi.

page 59

Vittorio Carpaccio. Venice, MUSEO CORRER. I. 2177, 2178. *Add:* from the dismembered polyptych of S. Frosca.
— Venice, CA'D'ORO. Annunciation and Death of the Virgin. *Add:* From the Scuola degli Albanesi.

page 113

Mazzola. Englewood. *Cancel completely.*

page 169

Tintoretto. Ex Lanz Collection, *now:* Amsterdam University, Loan from the Nederlands Kunstbezit.

CORRECTIONS TO THE PLATES

182. Vienna, Kunsthistorisches Museum (Lederer Gift).

485. Signed.

579. Art Institute.